Grand Prix Cookbook
Copyright © Neil Lewis 2021

Contents

Information and notes

Introduction	4
About the quirky bits	4
Useful information	4
Unit conversion	4
Common terms and symbols	5
Oven settings	5
For vegetarians and vegans	5

F1 2021 Race Calendar and Recipes

Bahrain (Sakhir)	28th March	6
Italy (Imola)	18th April	10
Portugal (Portimão)	2nd May	14
Spain (Barcelona)	9th May	18
Monaco (Monaco)	23rd May	22
Azerbaijan (Baku)	6th June	26
Canada (Montreal)	13th June	30
France (Le Castellet)	27th June	34
Austria (Spielberg)	4th July	38
Great Britain (Silverstone)	18th July	42
Hungary (Budapest)	1st August	46
Belgium (Spa)	29th August	50
Netherlands (Zandvoort)	5 September	54
Italy (Monza)	12th September	58
Russia (Sochi)	26th September	62
Singapore (Singapore)	3rd October	66
Japan (Suzuka)	10th October	70
USA (Austin)	24th October	74
Mexico (Mexico City)	31st October	78
Brazil (Sao Paulo)	7th November	82
Australia (Melbourne)	21st November	86
Saudi Arabia (Jeddah)	5th December	90
Abu Dhabi (Abu Dhabi)	12th December	94

Appendices

Appendix 1 - essentials	98
Appendix 2 - quote quiz	100
Alphabetical list of recipes	102

"You are not giving me useful information"

Introduction

When you visit a Grand Prix venue, there's usually a varied choice of street food to sustain you. Local street food can be an important part of the overall experience, especially for a race series like F1, where each race is held in a different country.

We can't all go to every race around the globe, so this book recreates that part of the experience in your own home.

Even if you're not an experienced cook, you'll find these recipes easy to make. They need no special equipment and avoid fiddly techniques. Where possible, they have been adapted if necessary to avoid ingredients which may be hard to find.

Like any other race fan, I don't like to spend race day in the kitchen. These recipes are mostly quick to make, or may be prepared in advance.

There are a few special dishes which need a bit more planning and effort. If those don't suit you, there are many others to choose from.

Note: There are almost no drinks or desserts in this book. Track side drinks mostly come in cans or bottles and deserts tend to be quite minimal. I'm fairly sure you can work those parts out yourself!

About the quirky bits

The racing car illustrations on the venue pages are in the national colours and driven by the national animal of each host country.

You'll also see boxed quotes. Try to work out who said what. The answers are in appendix 2.

Useful information

Most recipes in this book are for four adult portions, but may be easily scaled up or down.

Measures are mostly metric, but as a practical cook, I do use teaspoons (tsp) and tablespoons (tbs) too.

Unit conversion

The following conversions for US, Imperial and metric units are approximate.

Liquids

US	Imperial	Metric
1 tsp	1 tsp	5 ml
1 tbs	1 tbs	15 ml
⅛ cup	1 fl oz	30 ml
¼ cup	2 fl oz	60 ml
⅓ cup	2½ fl oz	80 ml
½ cup	4 fl oz	120 ml
1 cup	8 fl oz	240 ml

Most dry ingredients

US	Imperial	Metric
1 oz	1 oz	28 g
4 oz	4 oz	112 g
8 oz	8 oz	224 g
1 pound	16 oz	454 g

Plain Flour and bread flour

US	Imperial	Metric
¼ cup	1¼ oz	37g
⅓ cup	1¾ oz	50g
½ cup	2¾ oz	75g
1 cup	5¼ oz	150g

Wholemeal Flour

US	Imperial	Metric
¼ cup	1 oz	30g
⅓ cup	1½ oz	40g
½ cup	2 oz	60g
1 cup	4¼ oz	120g

Commonly used terms

Some ingredients and also the method of preparation for raw ingredients go by different names in various parts of the world.

Cooking terms

US	UK
broiled	grilled
ground	minced or chopped

Ingredients

US	UK
all purpose flour	plain flour
beet	beetroot
bell pepper	red or green pepper
cilantro	coriander leaf
cornmeal	polenta
cornstarch	cornflour
endive	chicory
eggplant	aubergine
heavy cream	double cream
light cream	single cream
plastic wrap	cling film
scallion	spring onion
skillet	frying pan
zucchini	courgette

Symbols

More hats = harder   More clocks = longer

Very easy   Very quick

Easy   Quick

Advanced      Slow

Oven settings

Fahrenheit	Celsius	Gas Mark
275	140	1
300	150	2
325	165	3
350	177	4
375	190	5
400	200	6
425	220	7
450	230	8
475	245	9
500	260	10

For vegetarians and vegans

Most recipes can be adapted for vegetarians and vegans quite easily.

Use alternatives such as tofu, soya mince or Quorn for minced or diced meat.

Quorn and tofu joints are now on sale and can be used to substitute for meat joints.

Specified cheeses can usually be replaced with vegan or rennet-free vegetarian alternatives.

A few recipes use whole eggs, which can be replaced with moulded tofu.

Eggs used in many other recipes can be replaced with aqua faba or simply omitted.

Bahrain

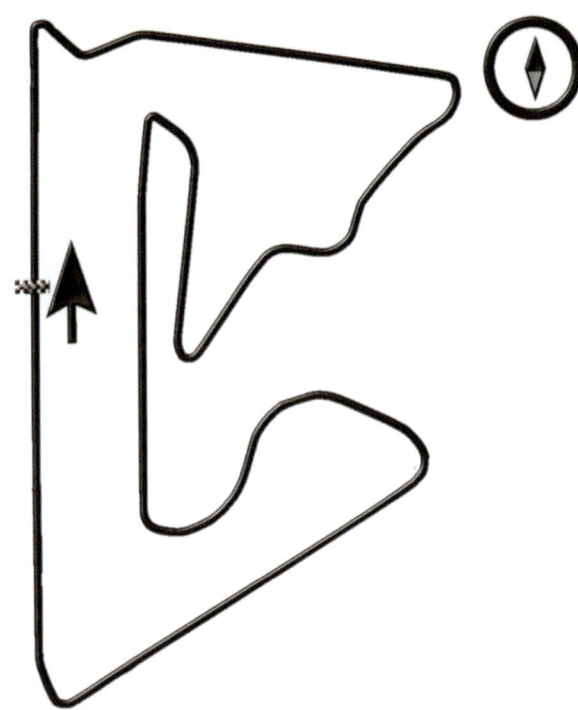

Bahrain International Circuit

Capacity 70,000
Length   5.027 Km (3.296 Miles)
Lap record Pedro De La Rosa(McLaren) 2005
            91.447 seconds

F1's first Middle East venue was built on a former camel farm, south of Manama.

The layout is typical of modern circuits, with long straights and slow corners. Setup is usually for medium downforce, with the track surface providing high grip levels.

Since it begins at dusk, conditions change from daylight to floodlit during the course of the race.

Sakhir

Sakhir is a desert area in the south of the Kingdom of Bahrain.

There are more than 30 islands which make up the Kingdom of Bahrain, the third smallest country in Asia.

It's unlikely to affect most visitors, but male gynaecologists must use a mirror to examine patients, because a man looking directly at a woman's genitals is strictly forbidden. Unless she's his wife, of course.

Some hotels may refuse entry to couples who do not appear to be married, and public displays of affection are likely to offend local people.

The Guinness Book of World Records has documented the world's largest coin toss event in Bahrain, organised by the British School of Bahrain. As part of World Maths Day in 2010, 1,117 staff and students took part in the toss.

Bahrain rejected a bid to ban the sale and consumption of pork. The government believed it would go against the wishes of the non-Muslim population of the country.

Roasted parsnip and hummus wraps

You will need

400g parsnips, peeled and chopped, 1 tbs olive oil, 25g spinach/rocket, 4 cloves garlic, 1 tsp honey, 125g hummus (see recipe in Abu Dhabi section) flat bread wraps, 125g grated mozzarella, salt and pepper to season.

Method

Preheat the oven to 200C/gas 6. Toss parsnips with garlic, olive oil, honey and seasoning. Place on a lined baking tray.

Roast 30-35 minutes, until parsnips are crispy outside, soft inside. Leave to cool.

Squeeze garlic from skins and mash, then stir into hummus.

Place wraps on a plate and spread with hummus. Add parsnips and spinach or rocket, then sprinkle with mozzarella. Roll up tightly and serve.

Slow-roast tomato, aubergine & feta

You will need

2 large, ripe tomatoes, 1 large aubergine, olive oil, 100g feta, rocket or baby spinach, salt, pepper.

Method

Cut tomatoes in half, add salt and olive oil and roast on the lowest setting overnight.

Cut aubergine into 1cm slices. Add salt, pepper and olive oil. Roast 10 mins at 200C/gas 6.

Mix together, sprinkle over feta and serve on a bed of rocket or baby spinach.

Watermelon and feta salad

You will need

500g coarsely chopped watermelon flesh,
1 coarsely chopped red onion,
100g feta, small bunch fresh mint.

Method

Layer onion, watermelon and feta in a bowl and garnish with sprigs of mint.

"Are we safe?
Can I go for a wee?"

Chicken machboos

You will need

175g basmati rice, 1 large onion,
350g chicken pieces - thighs or drumsticks, skinned, filleted or not,
1 large tomato, diced, 3-4 tbs coriander leaves,
1 green chilli, 1 lime,
ground spice mix as follows: ½ tsp black pepper, ½ tsp coriander, 1 tsp cinnamon, ½ tsp cloves, 1 tsp cumin, ½ tsp cardamom, ½ tsp nutmeg, ½ tsp paprika, 1 tsp turmeric, ½ tsp ginger.
1 clove garlic, finley chopped, 20g butter,
25ml lemon juice, 20ml rose water (if available)
25ml oil, 1 tsp salt, 500ml chicken stock.

Method

Mix ground spices and add 1 tsp salt. Sprinkle half of the spice mix on the chicken.

Chop and fry onions in a large pan until golden, add chilli. Quarter the lime and add to the mix. Add chicken and turn over a few times in the pan. Sprinkle with remaining spices and coat evenly. Cover and cook on medium heat for 3 mins.

Add garlic and diced tomato, mix, cover and cook 3 mins. Add remaining salt and 500ml water. Cover and cook 1 hour.

Add chopped coriander. Cook 5 mins.

Wash rice and soak for 10 mins, then drain.

Remove chicken from pan and place on baking tray, brush with oil and sprinkle with cinnamon powder, then bake or grill until golden brown.

Add rice to the stock, stir, then cook on low until the rice absorbs the stock.

Sprinkle rose water and lemon juice over rice and place the butter pieces on top.
Cover pan and cook on low until tender.

Serve the rice on a large serving plate and place the grilled chicken pieces on the top.

Roasted pumpkin

You will need

1 Pumpkin - size depends on how hungry you are!)
Olive oil. Salt, pepper, chopped coriander.

Method

Cut pumpkin to 1cm-2cm slices with the skin on.
Brush with olive oil and sprinkle with salt.
Roast in a hot oven for 10-15 minutes until tender, then sprinkle with pepper and coriander to garnish.

> "Racing drivers have balls.
> Unfortunately,
> none of them are crystal"

Beetroot and carrot salad

You will need

1 beetroot, grated, 2-3 carrots, grated, small bunch spring onions, chopped, 3 tbs chopped coriander, 1 lemon, olive oil, salt, pepper, 25g pomegranate seeds.

Method

Blanch the beetroot and carrot. Mix with the spring onion and chopped coriander.

Chop the lemon in half. Grate zest off one half and squeeze juice over the vegetables. Thinly slice the other half. Drizzle a little olive oil over the salad and season with salt and pepper. Sprinkle with pomegranate seeds and garnish with lemon zest.

Squash and aubergine dip

You will need

500g squash, 1 aubergine, 2 tbs tahini, 2 tbs sesame seeds, 1 clove garlic, chopped, juice of 1 lemon, 1 tsp olive oil, 125ml chopped parsley, salt.

Method

Peel squash, cut in small pieces. Steam, drain and mash coarsely. Pierce aubergine with fork, grill gently about 30 mins until evenly browned. Slit lengthwise, spoon out pulp and mix with squash. Add tahini, sesame seeds, garlic, lemon juice, parsley and salt. Serve with slices of pitta bread.

Yellow rice with meat

You will need

500g diced lamb or beef,
Ground spice mix as follows:
½ tsp black pepper, 1½ tsp cumin, 1½ tsp turmeric, ½ tsp coriander, 1 tsp cinnamon, ½ tsp cloves, ½ tsp nutmeg, ½ tsp paprika, ½ tsp ginger, ½ tsp cardamom.
2 tomatoes sliced, 1 pepper, diced, 2 onions, sliced, few large cabbage leaves, 2 cloves garlic, sliced, 500g basmati rice, 50g raisins, olive oil, pinch of saffron, 1 sliced lemon to garnish.

Method

Soak rice and raisins separately in water for at least 30 mins. Rub ground spices over meat, let stand 15 mins, then brown well.

Preheat oven to 180C/gas 4. Line oven dish with half the cabbage. Add half the tomato, onion, peppers, garlic, then the meat, then the remaining tomato, onion, peppers and garlic. Cover with remaining cabbage.

Bake until tender, 2-3 hours. Remove meat and put vegetables in a pot. Add drained rice, enough water to cover and salt to taste. Sprinkle with saffron and raisins. Cover and cook on low heat for 15 mins.

Serve meat pieces on rice and garnish with the lemon slices.

Italy - Imola

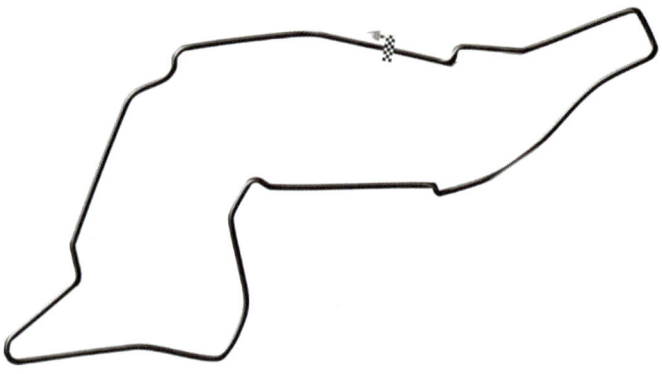

Autodromo Internazionale Enzo e Dino Ferrari

Capacity 60,000
Length 4.909 Km (3.050 Miles)
Lap record Lewis Hamilton (Mercedes) 2020
 75.484 seconds

The circuit, situated on the edge of the small town of Imola, about 40Km easy of Bologna, is one of the few major international circuits to run in an anti-clockwise direction. It used to feature regularly in F1 as the San Marino Grand Prix.

The gradual addition of chicanes over the years has changed it's original character from that of a high speed, low downforce track to a medium/high downforce track, with high cornering speeds.

Imola

The Autodromo Enzo e Dino Ferrari is located in the Emilia Romagna region, on the southern outskirts of the city of Imola in north-central Italy. Imola itself is close to the A14 highway, linking it to Bologna and Modena

There are a lot of Medieval castles and Renaissance palaces in Emilia Romagna. Some of the best-preserved are in Parma and Piacenza. Some are open to overnight guests.

Europe's oldest university is in Bologna, in the heart of the region. Founded in 1088, notable alumni include Giorgio Armani, Guglielmo Marconi.

You'll also find the factories of Ferrari, Lamborghini, Ducati, and Maserati, as well as 11 motoring museums and various impressive car collections.

The region's culinary claims to fame include prosciutto di Parma, Parmigiano Reggiano, and the traditional aged balsamic vinegar of Modena. It's known for generous seasonings, olives, meats, fish, salami, and cheeses, and also for the variety and quality of pasta.

Strozzapreti ("priest-choker" or "priest-strangler"), is one of the most famous and widespread pasta shapes from Emilia Romagna. The name comes from the way the pasta is twisted to obtain the traditional shape.

Fresh Egg Pasta

You will need

4 large eggs,
400g type '00' flour, or plain flour if unavailable

Method

Put the flour in a large bowl, make a well in the center and crack the eggs into it. Beat with a fork, then mix well to make a smooth dough.

Alternatively, put everything into a food processor and mix to a breadcrumb-like texture. Then remove the dough and knead until firm and smooth.

Wrap dough in clingfim and refrigerate one hour.

Divide the dough evenly into four pieces. Roll each piece out on a flat, floured surface.

How thick you need your pasta depends upon what you're making with it. For strips, e.g. tagliatelli, lasagne, etc. roll it about 2mm thick. For making stuffed pasta shapes, about 1mm thick or less.

Cut or shape your pasta as needed. If you leave it out for more than an hour or so, it'll go very dry and brittle - a bit like bought dried pasta - but you can cook it straight away without drying.

For variations, add a little tomato puree, finely chopped spinach or fresh herbs.

To make coloured pasta, add the tomato (red) or the spinach (green) and knead it into the dough before leaving it to chill in the refrigerator.

If adding fresh herbs, do so while rolling out the pasta, by sprinkling on the surface, then folding the pasta over and rolling again.

Ragù
(Savoury meat sauce for pasta)

You will need

600g minced beef (or 300g each minced beef and pork), 100g minced bacon.
Optionally, 100g each of any combination of smoked ham, chicken livers or Italian sausage.
Chopped vegetables: 1 medium onion, 1 carrot, 1 stick celery. Approx 75-100ml red wine,
1 tbs chopped fresh basil, 1 tsp dried oregano,
300g canned tomatoes, blended to a puree,
200ml meat or vegetable stock, 100ml milk,

240g dried pasta (spaghetti or tagliatelli) or make fresh pasta using the recipe in the previous panel.

Grated parmesan cheese to serve.

Method

Heat some olive oil in a large, oven proof pan and gently fry the celery, carrot and onion until soft.

Stir in the meat and fry until evenly browned.

Add the red wine, stock, milk and herbs and simmer gently until it reduces to a thick sauce - this could take a couple of hours. Season to taste.

Meanwhile. cook the fresh or dried pasta in plenty of boiling salted water for about ten minutes, then drain it well.

Serve pasta on a large plate or bowl and add the Ragù on top, then sprinle with grated parmesan.

> "Can you describe conditions around the track, please?"
>
> "Errr, f***ing wet!"

Lasagne verde al forno
(Green lasagne bake)

You will need

1 recipe fresh egg pasta with spinach (page 11) left as sheets, each about 20cm long x 10cm wide.
1 recipe Ragù (page 11)

Bechamel sauce: 40g butter, 2 tbs plain flour, 500ml warm milk, a pinch ground nutmeg.

Cheese: 90g grated parmesan, 600g ricotta, 60g melted butter.

Method

Bechamel: While the ragu is simmering, combine 40g butter and 2 tbs flour in a saucepan over low heat. Stir or whisk to make a smooth sauce. Remove from heat and let rest one minute, then whisk in warm milk. Return to heat and simmer for 10 mins, stirring until thickened, then add salt and nutmeg and remove from heat.

Pasta: Boil the pasta sheets a few at a time in plenty of salted water for about three mins, then remove them and drop into cold (or preferably iced) water for a few moments, then drain and dry.

Preheat oven to 200C.

To assemble the lasagna, place one pasta sheet in the bottom of a greased baking dish.

Spread 1/3 of the ragu, 1/4 of the bechamel, 1/3 of the ricotta and 1/4 of the parmesan over the pasta.

Repeat layers twice, then top with remaining bechamel and parmesan and dot with butter.

Bake in the preheated oven for 30 mins, until the top is golden brown.

Mortadella, fig and asiago sandwich

You will need (per person)

Two slices Italian bread, e.g. ciabata,
3-4 slices mortadella, 2-3 fresh figs* sliced thinly,
1 thick slice asiago or crumbly maturte cheddar.

Place the cheese on a slice of bread. Add the mortadella, folding each piece over into an 'S' shape, so it forms multi-layered ribbon of meat.

Now place the sliced figs on top of the meat and finally add the second slice of bread.

Toast the assembled sandwich until it's golden brown and the cheese starts to melt. Serve.

*Fresh figs are not always available, but they do freeze remarkably well. Buy when in season and keep frozen until you need them. Don't try to use dried figs - the flavour and texture are both completely different!

Tortellini al Brodo
(Stuffed pasta soup)

You will need

1 recipe fresh egg pasta (page 11) rolled to about 3mm thick and cut in 40mm squares. Cover the pasta squares to keep them moist.

Broth: 500g chicken, diced, 250g veal bones, 250g diced stewing beef, 1 stick celery, chopped, 1 onion, quartered, 1 carrot, coarsely chopped, about 20g Parmigiano-Reggiano rind (optional)

Filling: 2 tsp melted butter, 40g diced pork loin, 30ml dry white wine, 30g chopped prosciutto, 30g chopped mortadella, 10g grated parmesan, pinch of grated nutmeg, 1 small egg, lightly beaten.

Method

Broth: Put all broth ingredients in a large pot and add 1500ml cold water. Cover and bring to simmer over medium heat, then reduce heat to low. Skim off any foam from the surface. Simmer gently for about 2 ½ hours, adding salt to taste.

Remove chicken and save the meat for another use. Discard the other solids from the broth and strain through a strainer lined with cheesecloth or kitchen towel into a large bowl. Refrigerate overnight in a sealed container. Remove fat and reserve broth.

Filling: Melt butter over medium heat and cook the pork, stirring, until lightly golden. Increase heat to high, add wine, and stir until almost evaporated. Transfer pork and juices to a food processor. Add prosciutto and mortadella and process until very finely chopped, but not puréed.

Transfer filling to a bowl and add the parmesan, nutmeg, egg, and a pinch of salt. Mix well. Cover the bowl and refrigerate.

Tortellini: Put about 1/8 tsp. of the filling in the center of a pasta square. Bring one corner over the filling toward the corner diagonally opposite and fold into a triangle. Press around the filling to seal.

Bend the tortellino around your finger with one corner slightly overlapping the other and press to seal. The tortellino will look like a crown.

Transfer to a large baking tray lined with clean kitchen towel. Arrange the tortellini in a single layer without letting them touch and cover with another clean towel to keep from drying out.

To serve: Bring the broth to a boil in a large pot over medium heat. Gently drop the tortellini into the pot. Cook until they rise to the surface and are tender but still firm to the bite. This will take about 2 to 3 minutes. Remove the pot from the heat and ladle the tortellini and broth into serving bowls. Sprinkle with grated Parmigiano, and serve.MortadellaM

> "Holy f***,
> I'm hanging here like a cow!"

Portugal

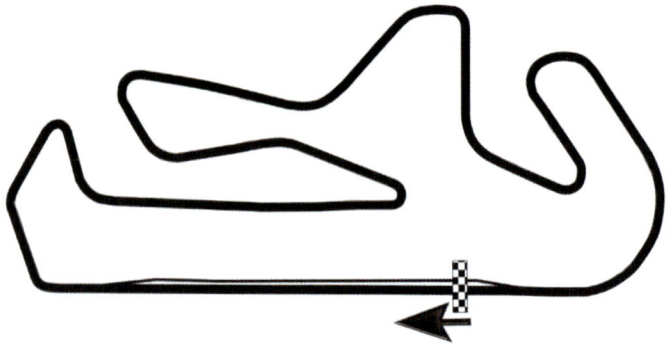

Algarve International Circuit, Portimão

Capacity	100,000
Length	4.653 Km (2.891 Miles)
Lap record	Lewis Hamilton (Mercedes) 2020 78.750 seconds

The track constantly undulates, in a similar way to Spa. There are big downhill slopes and right hand turns after the main straight. The width of the track makes it good for overtaking. Despite only being completed in 2008, the circuit is said to feel a bit dangerous, similar to some of the older, more traditional circuits, with many corners having a distinct personality.

The 2020 coronavirus pandemin resulted in the circuit hosting a Portuguese F1 race for the first time since 1996

Portimão

Portimão is the largest city in the western Algarve region of southern Portugal. Traditionally a centre for shipbuilding and sardine fishing, it's now a popular tourist spot, known for its old quarter, busy marina and the nearby beaches at Praia de Rocha.

The old fish docks have been transformed into a scenic promenade, while the city itself boasts quaint traditional plazas, historic buildings and many cafes and bars, as well as restaurants specialising in seafood dishes.

The Museu de Portimão is housed in the old Feu Cannery and presents the history of an industry which boomed here in the early 20th century.

In addition to F1, the Autódromo Internacional do Algarve hosts the Superbike World Championship and the Le Mans Series.

During the week, you can come for "track days" taking a racing bike or supercharged sportscar out for a spin, or taking a racing lesson from a pro.

There's also a karting track at the circuit that can cater to children as young as nine.

It's seen as bad form to eat while walking in the street. You may buy food in a fast food place or at a vending machine, but do not to parade down the road eating it as people may take offence.

Conversely, the Portuguese are big fans of public drinking until the small hours of the morning. This nightlife culture is very different from the civilised daytime rules, so be prepared to adapt to both.

Most Portuguese speak good English, but tend to be very shy about this ability. They're not being deliberately difficult, just really modest.

Chunky cod fritters with aïoli

You will need

Fish: 200g potatoes, 250g skinless cod fillet, milk for poaching, 2 tbsp chopped coriander, 1 large shallot or small onion, finely chopped, 3 tbsp port wine, a pinch of grated nutmeg, 3 medium eggs, beaten, 150g coarse breadcrumbs, 2tbsp plain flour, plus more for dusting, lemon wedges to serve.
Aïoli: 2 egg yolks, 15g Dijon mustard, 1 lemon, zested and juiced, 1 garlic clove, crushed, 400ml vegetable oil.

Method

Make the aïoli by putting the egg yolks, mustard, garlic, lemon zest and juice in a small blender and blend to a smooth paste. With the motor still running, slowly add the oil: drop by drop to begin with, then, when it starts to thicken, add the oil a little faster until you have a thick, smooth mixture. Season with salt and cover.

Boil the potatoes whole with skin on. Drain and leave to cool, then peel them with your fingers. Dice half the potatoes and mash the other half.

Put the cod in a pan, cover with milk and poach for a few minutes, until cooked. Drain and flake the cod with your hands.

Mix potatoes, cod, coriander, shallots, and port in a bowl and season with salt, pepper and nutmeg. Add 1 beaten egg and 2 tbsp of flour to bind the mixture and form into 8 squares or balls by hand, then chill them for 30 minutes until firm.

Put the remaining 2 beaten eggs in one bowl with the breadcrumbs in another. Dust the chilled fish and potato fritters with flour, then coat in the egg and breadcrumbs.

Heat 3cm-4cm of oil in a large frying pan until hot but not smoking. Fry the fritters a few minutes on each side until crisp, and cooked through, then drain on kitchen paper and serve with a dollop of aïoli and a wedge of lemon.

Portuguese seafood rice

You will need

1 **onion, finely chopped**, 2 tbs olive oil,
2 **celery sticks, finely chopped**,
1 **tbs paprika, 6 large cloves garlic, crushed.**
2 **bay leaves**, ½ **tsp dried chilli flakes**,
4 **tomatoes, cored and roughly chopped**,
1 **400g can chopped tomatoes**,
1 **tsp granulated sugar, 100g risotto rice**,
750g **mussels, cleaned**, half a small bunch each of chopped oregano and chopped parsley,
200g large, raw king prawns, **25g butter, diced**.

Method

Cook onion and celery in the oil in a casserole over medium-high heat for 10 minutes or until softened. Add garlic and bay leaves. Cook until the garlic is translucent, then stir in paprika, chilli flakes and fresh tomatoes and season well.

Add tinned tomatoes and sugar with 1.5 litres of cold water, stir and cover with a lid. Bring to a simmer over medium heat, then reduce to low heat and simmer gently for 45 minutes.

Add the rice to the pot, stir once and leave to cook for 15 minutes on low heat with the lid on. Adjust seasoning, then add mussels, stir well replace the lid.

Cook for 10 minutes or until all of the mussels have opened (discard any that haven't). Add a little boiing water if the mixture looks dry, then add the prawns.

Replace the lid and cook for 2 minutes, then stir in the chopped oregano, parsley and butter. Serve in shallow bowls.

> "F*** me — that took quite a while, that! More than eighty races!"

Bifana
(Pork steak in a roll)

You will need

200ml white wine, 1 tbsp white wine vinegar,
1 tbs chargrilled red pepper paste, 2 tbsp olive oil,
3 garlic cloves, finely chopped, 1 tsp chilli flakes,
3 onions, thinly sliced, 1 tbs smoked paprika,
4 thin-cut pork loin steaks, 4 ciabatta rolls,
80g Italian-style salad, 2 tbs American mustard.

Method

Mix 150ml of the wine, the pepper paste, wine vinegar, paprika and garlic in a bowl. Season with salt and pepper to taste. Add the pork steaks coat well. Cover and chill for 5 hours, or overnight.

Heat 1 tbs oil in a large frying pan over medium heat. Add the onions and coat them in the oil, then reduce heat to low and leave to cook 30-35 mins until tender and golden. Stir occasionally to prevent the onions sticking to the pan.

Use the remaining wine and to deglaze the pan, then add the chilli flakes and cook for a 1 min. Remove the onions and set aside.

Wipe the pan clean and add 1 tbs oil over medium heat. Remove pork from the marinade and shake off any excess. Add the pork steaks to the pan and cook for 3 mins each side until nicely charred. Remove from the pan and drain.

Slice the ciabatta rolls in half, add salad, pork, onions and mustard to serve.Caldo VerdeCaldo

Caldo Verde
(Portuguese cabbage soup)

You will need

2 large onions, finely chopped, 1 chorizo sausage,
4 cloves garlic, crushed, 60ml olive oil,
6 large potatoes, diced, 1.5 litres vegetable stock,
2 bay leaves, large bunch of greens or cabbage,
some smoked paprika and olive oil.

Method

Heat some oil over low heat in a frying pan and fry onions and garlic until soft and translucent.

Chop the chorizo into small chunks and add to the pan and fry for a few more minutes. Add potatoes and continue frying until lightly browned.

Transfer the mixture to a large saucepan, add the stock and bay leaves, season with salt and pepper and continue to cook until the potatoes are soft. When the potatoes are ready, mash them into the broth to thicken the soup.

Meanwhile, chop the cabbage very finely. Blanch the greens in boiling water for one minute, then drain and add to the broth - if you want heavy soup add loads of greens, if lighter, add less.

Simmer for a few minutes. Mix the smoked paprika with some olive oil to make a dressing and stir this into the green soup.

Serve the soup with some rustic country bread.

> *"What a crazy start!*
> *What are they doing?*
> *They need to calm down"*

Peri-Peri Chicken with crispy potatoes

You will need

1500g chicken,
600g red potatoes, sliced 8mm thick.

Marinade: 2 dried red chillies - peri-peri or similar, 2 tbs smoked paprika, 6 cloves garlic, 1 tbs salt,
1 tsp ground coriander, 60ml lemon juice,
75ml sherry vinegar, 75ml olive oil, black pepper.

Sauce: 250g plain yogurt, ½ teaspoon salt,
1 bunch coriander leaves, finely chopped
½ tsp ground coriander, cracked black pepper,
1 tbs lemon juice, 1 tbs olive oil.

Method

Preheat oven to 230C or as close as you can get! Soak dried chilies in hot for 20 minutes.

Blend the marinade ingredients into a paste. Brush a layer of marinade onto a flat baking pan.

Place the potatoes on top of the marinade. Allow them to overlap slightly. Sprinkle with salt.

Brush marinade all over the chicken pieces, coating fairly heavily. Place chicken, skin side down on the potatoes and place in the hot oven.

Every 15 mins, turn chicken over, brush with marinade and return to the oven. Repeat until the chicken is cooked - about 45-60 mins, depending on the size of the pieces.

Remove the chicken and set it aside for 5-10 mins.

Meanwhile, continue to roast the potatoes or grill them until crisp and golden.

Combine the sauce ingredients in a bowl or food processor. Serve the chicken and potatoes and put the sauce in a separate dish.

Francesinha sandwich

You will need

Filling: 2 plain sausages, 2 smoked sausages,
2 thin steaks, 4 slices bread, 10 slices melty cheese
4 slices ham or salami, 2 eggs.
Sauce: 2 chopped onions 2 bay leaves,
1-2 tbs diced bacon, 500 ml passata, chilli flakes,
330 ml beer, 175 ml white wine,
4 cloves garlic, crushed, 2 oz butter,
500 ml beef or chicken stock,
milk and flour for thickening.

Method

Cut sausages lengthwise and season with salt and pepper. Season the steaks. Grill sausages, then the steaks.

For the sauce, chop the onions and garlic and fry gently in the butter and olive oil, with the bay leaves and bacon. Add passata and some chillies to taste and bring to a fast simmer. Add beer, winei and stock. Simmer 20 minutes.

Mix milk and flour with a fork and stir into the sauce. Remove bay leaves and blend sauce until smooth.

Assemble your francesinha by layering a slice of bread, one slice of cheese, one of salami, the steak and the sausages, then a second slice of bread. Repeat for the second sandwich.

Cover the sandwiches with the remaining sliced cheese bake or grill until it melts.

Fry eggs and place one on top of each sandwich, then pour the hot sauce over and around.

Serve with french fries.

Spain

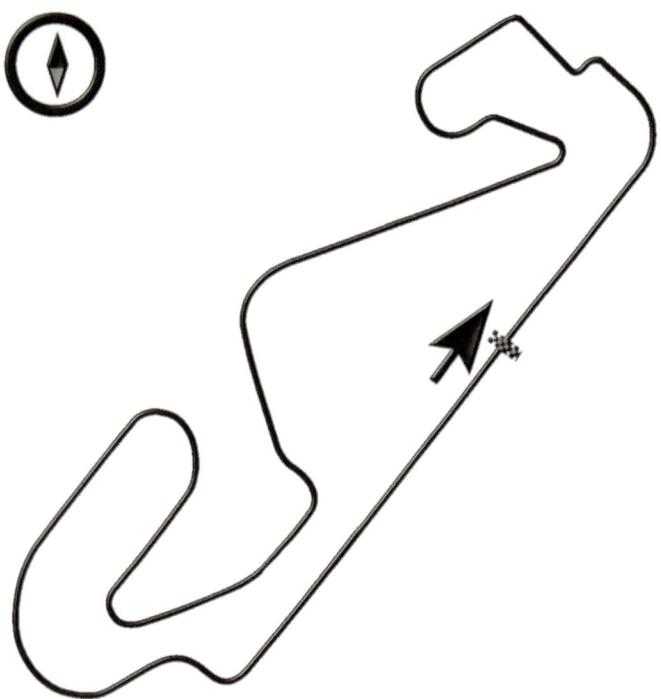

Circuit de Barcelona-Catalunya

Capacity	140,700
Length	4.655 Km (4.892 Miles)
Lap record	D Ricciardo (Red Bull) 2018 78.441 seconds

The Spanish Grand Prix has been hosted at the Circuit de Barcelona since it was built in 1991. It's used extensively for testing, so drivers are very familiar with its quirks.

Wind direction here can change drastically during race day, leading to unexpected performance problems.

Most overtaking happens in the braking zone for turn 1, after the long, DRS-enabled start-finish straight.

Barcelona

Barcelona is the capital of Spain's Catalonia region. Famed for its art and architecture, the Sagrada Família church, Casa Batlló, Casa Milà and other modernist landmarks were designed by Antoni Gaudí for the city.

During the Spanish Civil War from 1936 to 1939, more than 1,000 bomb shelters were built beneath Barcelona. Some are in stations, others beneath the streets, and some are even in people's back gardens.

There were no good public beaches in Barcelona until 1992. What is now the seaside of Barcelona was once full of local industries until the city was chosen to host the Olympic Games.

One of Barcelona's most famous traditions involves people forming human castles. Castellers, as they're known, practise this official sport at the weekend and during holidays and festivals throughout the year.

The caganer, or 'crapper', is a Christmas tradition. As families decorate their nativity scene, no figure is as important as the peasant dropping his pants somewhere near the animals and other characters.

Sweet chilli pork belly tapas

You will need

500g pork belly slices, 1 apple, 1 onion, 3 tomatoes, 1 tsp pimentón or paprika, 2 dried chillies, 50g sugar, salt, olive oil.

Method

Chop onions, chillies, tomatoes and apple. Fry onion and chillies in a little oil, then add tomatoes and apple, sugar, paprika and pinch of salt. Simmer 5-10 mins.

Score the skin on the pork belly with a sharp knife into small squares. Don't cut right through!

Put the onion, tomato and chilli mixture into an ovenproof dish and arrange the belly slices on top, keeping them together.

Cover and bake for 2 hours at 120C/gas ½. Uncover and cook 1 hour at 150C/gas 2.

Remove the pork and chop into cubes.

Transfer sauce to pan and reduce until it thickens. Add 1 tsp cornflour if necessary.

Mix the pork back into the sauce and serve.

Spanish omelette (Tortilla)

You will need

500g waxy potatoes, 60ml olive oil, 4 garlic cloves, 1 onion, 2 tbs chopped parsley, salt, ground black pepper, 6 eggs.

Method

Peel potatoes and cut into 1cm slices. Peel and thinly slice onion and garlic.

Parboil the potato slices for about 5 minutes, then drain and set aside.

Heat the oil in a deep sided non-stick pan over medium heat. Add the onion and garlic and cook until softened.

Add the potato slices and parsley and mix well, then cover. Cook over medium heat for 5 mins, gently pressing down into the pan.

Whisk the eggs with 1 tsp salt and black pepper, then pour evenly over potato mixture.

Cover and cook over very low heat for 20 mins until the eggs are set.

Carefully slide out onto plate to serve.

"Don't talk to me through the corners"

Broad beans with ham

You will need

10g butter, 1 garlic clove, crushed,
100g chopped jamón or prosciutto,
1 small chopped onion, 250g broad beans,
70ml dry white wine, 100ml chicken stock,
salt, black pepper.

Method

Fry onion, jamón and garlic in butter at medium heat for about 5 mins.

Add broad beans and wine. Cook at high heat. Add stock and reduce heat to low. Cover and cook for 10 mins. Uncover and simmer for 10 mins until the beans are tender and the mixture is fairly dry.

Serve hot with crusty bread.

Sangria

You will need

1½ tbs caster sugar, 1 tbs lemon juice,
1 tbs orange juice, 1 bottle red wine,
500ml lemonade, 2 tbs gin, 1 tbs vodka, 1 lemon,
1 orange, 1 lime, ice cubes.

Method

Mix the sugar, lemon juice and orange juice in a jug and stir thoroughly to dissolve.

Add all the other liquid ingredients. Halve the fruit, remove seeds and slice thinly.

Add to pitcher with ice cubes and stir well.

Albóndigas
(Pork meatballs in a spicy sauce)

You will need

Meatballs: 175g minced pork, 175g minced beef,
3 cloves garlic, 35g breadcrumbs, 1 tsp ground cumin,
1 tsp ground coriander, 1 tsp ground nutmeg,
1 pinch ground cinnamon, 2 tbs olive oil,
1 whisked egg.

Sauce: 1 tbs olive oil, 1 onion, chopped,
2 garlic cloves, 125ml dry white wine,
400g can chopped tomatoes, 1 tbs tomato puree,
125ml chicken stock, ½ tsp chilli powder,
80g frozen or fresh peas.

Method

Mix pork, beef, chopped garlic, spices, egg. Season and mix in breadcrumbs until smooth, then refrigerate 30 mins. Roll into small balls.

Toss the balls a few at a time in olive oil over medium heat until browned. Drain.

For the sauce, fry the onions at medium heat until translucent. Add garlic and cook for 1 min.

Add tomatoes, puree and stock and simmer 10 mins until it thickens.

Add meatballs to sauce, heat through thoroughly and serve hot.

Gazpacho
(Chilled vegetable soup)

You will need

1 red onion, chopped, 2 garlic cloves, minced,
1 red pepper, deseeded and chopped, 4 tomatoes,
1 slice white bread, crusts removed, 500ml passata,
300ml vegetable stock, 5 tbs olive oil,
4 tbs wine vinegar, 1 tsp Tabasco or harissa,
1 tsp sugar, basil leaves, to serve.

Method
Blend onion, garlic, pepper, tomatoes and bread in a food processor until chopped, but not too smooth.

Tip into a bowl with passata, stock, oil, vinegar, Tabasco, sugar and season to taste. Mix, cover and refrigerate 2hrs or overnight.

Serve in small bowls, drizzled with olive oil and sprinkled with torn basil.

Migas
(Fried breadcrumbs with ham)

You will need
1 small loaf of bread, chopped in 5mm cubes,
1 garlic bulb, 1 tbs paprika,
200g serrano ham or bacon, 2 slices bread,
60ml olive oil, salt.

Method

Wrap bread cubes s in moist cloth overnight.

Cut ham or bacon and sliced bread in 10mm dice.

Fry ham or bacon in the oil. Remove and drain.

Add garlic cloves without peeling, fry lightly, then remove and drain.

Brown the diced bread in the same oil, remove and drain. Add more oil if necessary, 1 tsp of paprika and the finely chopped bread. Remove when they start to change colour.

Add the ham or bacon and the croutons.

Escalivada
(Grilled vegetables with bread)

You will need

1 aubergine, 2 red peppers, chopped parsley, anchovy fillets, olive oil, sliced ripe tomato, some pieces of crusty bread.

Method
Slowly grill the aubergine and peppers until the skin is evenly blackened. Cool, peel skin and slice lengthwise.

Serve with the garnishes and bread.

> "I'll try to contain my competitiveness so I don't come across like a dickhead"

Monaco

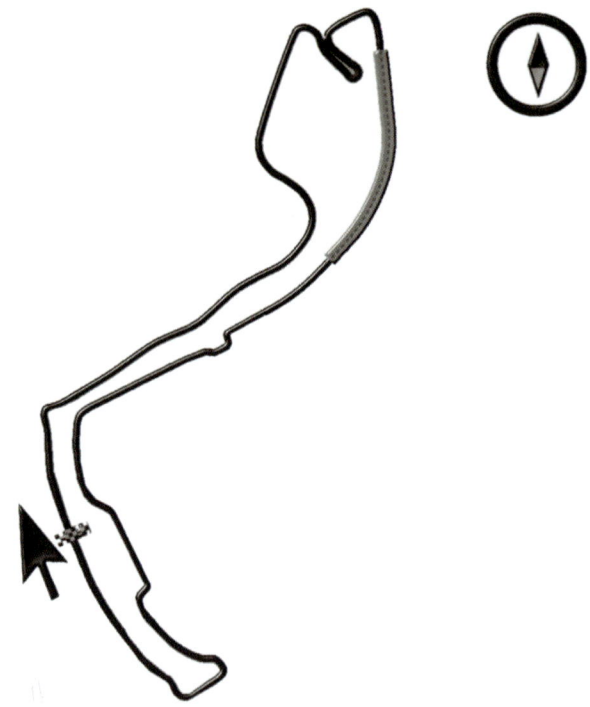

Circuit de Monaco

Capacity	37,000
Length	3.337 Km (2.074 Miles)
Lap record	M Verstappen(Red Bull) 2018 74.260 seconds

The tight, twisty circuit favours driving skill over power. There is little overtaking as the course is so narrow. The smallest of errors usually results in hitting the barriers.

It is generally recognised as less safe than other circuits. Were it not an established Grand Prix, it could not be added to the Formula One schedule, for safety reasons.

Setup is low downforce. Engine cooling and brake and tyre warming are problematic.

Monte-Carlo

Monaco is an independent city-state on France's Mediterranean coastline, with a population of just 37,800, of whom Monaco locals make up just 6,000. The rest are French, Italians, and people of around 125 other nationalities resident in Monaco.

Monte-Carlo is mainly known for casinos, its harbour and the prestigious and long running F1 Grand Prix motor race.

The town is home to a belle-époque casino complex, even though citizens of Monaco are not allowed to gamble, nor even visit the casinos.

Beware if taking a camera. Although the town is swamped with CCTV, use of a camera on the street is prohibited without a License to Shoot. Even that doesn't cover general photography, with individual permits being needed for most locations.

The economy is driven by radio, television and the casino and state monopolies on stamps and tobacco, plus banking and financial activities.

Pissaladière monégasque
(Pizza with onion and anchovies)

You will need

Base: 200g strong white bread flour, 1 tsp salt, 2 tsp easy blend dried yeast, 150ml warm water, 1 tbs olive oil.

Topping: 4 tbs olive oil, 1kg onion, thinly sliced, a few sprigs of thyme, handful of black olives, 2 tomatoes, skinned and chopped, 2x80g anchovy fillets.

Method

Mix flour, salt and yeast in a bowl. Add water and oil to mix to a soft dough. Turn out to lightly floured surface and knead 5 mins until smooth. Put in a lightly oiled bowl, then cover and leave 1 hour to rise.

Fry onions gently in a pan for 10 mins until soft, stirring occasionally. Add thyme and tomatoes, then season to taste. Mix, cover and cook gently for about 45 mins until soft. Leave to stand.

Meanwhile, preheat oven 220C/gas 7

Lightly oil a baking tray. Knead the dough briefly, then roll out and press into the tin.

Spread onion mixture over dough, arrange anchovies on top in a lattice pattern.

Add an olive in each 'window', then bake 25-30 mins until golden. Serve warm or cold.

Pasta & Potatoes with Provolone

You will need

200g pasta of various shapes, 60ml olive oil, 1 stalk celery, coarsely chopped, 1 onion, coarsely chopped, 1 sprig of rosemary, 2 potatoes, boiled, peeled and coarsely chopped, 120g provolone del Monaco or mature Cheddar.

Method

Cook pasta in boiling, salted water for 5 minutes.

Heat oil in a pan, add the celery and onions and fry until the onions are translucent. Add potatoes and enough water to cover.

Add the pasta and cook until the mixture thickens, about 15 mins. Season to taste.

Cut eight thin slices of cheese and grate the rest.

Add grated cheese to the potatoes and pasta and mix well.

Serve in 4 bowls, each garnished with 2 cheese slices and a sprig of rosemary.

"Just leave me alone, I know what I'm doing"

Antipasto della casa
(Cheese and bacon appetiser)

You will need

Salad: ½ iceberg lettuce, ½ romaine lettuce, 1 cucumber, 2 tomatoes, all diced.

Topping: 6 strips streaky bacon, well cooked, drained and crumbled, Cheddar cheese, cubed or sliced into small pieces.

Dressing: 125ml mayonnaise, 90ml milk, 125ml sour cream or yoghurt, 1 tbs lemon juice, 1 tbs chopped chives, 4-5 tbs chopped parsley, 1 clove garlic, finely chopped, 3 tbs Cheddar, 2 tsp red wine vinegar, 4 spring onions, sliced, black pepper.

Method

Dressing: Mix milk and lemon juice and set aside for about 5 mins.

Mix with the rest of the dressing ingredients and put aside for a few hours or overnight.

Mix salad ingredients and add dressing. Top with cheese and crumbled bacon.

Oignons monégasques
(Sweet-sour onions with herbs)

You will need

500-700g small onions, 300ml water, bouquet garni (bundled thyme, bay leaf, leafy celery top, parsley), 3 tbs olive oil, 2 tbs red wine vinegar, 4 tbs raisins, 2 tbs tomato puree, 1 tbs sugar, salt & pepper.

Method

Top and tail onions and place in a large heat-proof bowl. Cover with boiling water and set aside 10 mins. Drain onions and remove skins. Cut a cross at root end of each onion.

Fry onions gently in a large pan for 5 mins, stirring frequently. Add remaining ingredients, bring mixture to a simmer, cover and cook on low heat for 30 mins, stirring occasionally.

Uncover and simmer 15 mins to let sauce thicken. Stir to prevent sticking. Sauce should be thick and onions tender.

Adjust vinegar and sugar to sweet-sour. Allow to cool and remove bouquet garni.

"Driving in Monte Carlo is like riding a bike in your house"

Barbagiuan
(Deep-fried pastry appetiser)

You will need

Pastry: 210g plain flour, ½ tsp salt, 60ml olive oil, 1 large beaten egg, plus 1 beaten egg white for sealing, 3 tbs water.

Filling: 1½ tsp olive oil,
2 tbs onion, finely chopped,
2 tbs leeks (white part only), finely chopped,
2 Swiss chard leaves, shredded and chopped,
50g chopped fresh spinach,
½ tsp dried oregano, 2½ tbs ricotta,
1 tbs grated parmesan.

Method

Pastry: Sift flour and salt into bowl, add olive oil and 2 tbs of the beaten egg. Blend with fork and add water to make a firm dough.

Turn out to floured surface. Knead until smooth. Wrap in clingfilm and chill for 30 mins.

Filling: Heat oil and fry onion and leek over medium heat for 5 mins.

Add chard, spinach and oregano. Fry until chard is tender. Transfer to bowl.

Add cheese and remaining beaten egg from the pastry ingredients. Season and set aside to cool.

Roll dough to 2mm thick. Use a 6cm cutter to make as many rounds as you can, re-rolling as needed to make about 20 circles.

Put 1-2 tsp of filling in the middle of each pastry round, brush edges with egg white and fold over to form a semicircle. Press edges with a fork to seal.

Pour vegetable oil into a deep pan and heat to 190C. Add the pastries to the oil a few at a time, frying until brown and crisp. Transfer with a slotted spoon to a plate lined with kitchen towels.

Serve warm or at room temperature.

Socca
(Chickpea flatbread)

You will need

250g chickpea or gram flour, olive oil, 300ml water, salt and pepper for seasoning.

Method

Mix flour, 3 tbs olive oil, water and salt in a food processor until smooth.

Brush a large pan generously with oil and place on medium high heat. Pour enough batter to cover pan surface about 2mm thick. Season to taste with salt and pepper.

Cook until bottom is lightly browned and top is dry to the touch, 3-4 minutes.

Azerbaijan

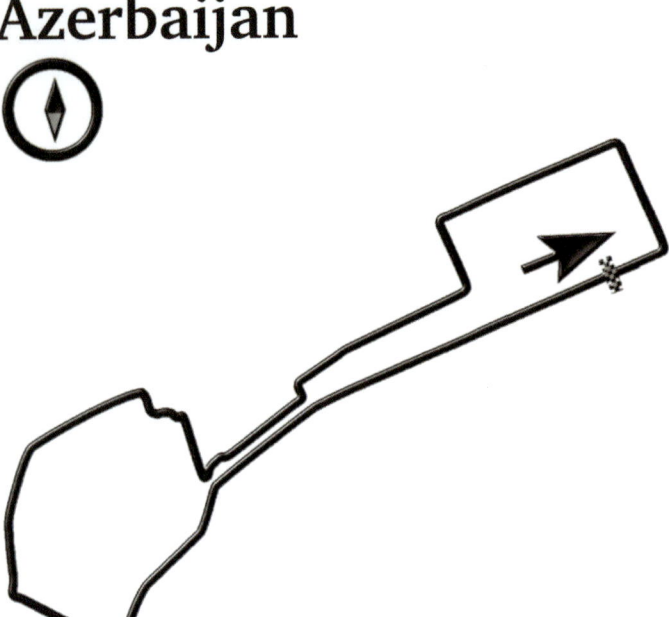

Baku City Circuit

Capacity	18,500
Length	6.003 Km (3.730 Miles)
Lap record	C LeClerc (Ferrari) 2019
	103.009 seconds

The first race at F1's second longest circuit was in 2016. With the longest flat out section of any F1 track, but also a highly technical section and very limited run off areas, there were pre-race safety concerns.

The 2016 race was uneventful, but 2017 provided a dizzying mix of crashes and entertaining track action. The 2017 result was arguably decided by an error at Mercedes, forcing Hamilton to pit from the lead to replace a loose head restraint.

Baku

Baku is the capital city and commercial hub of Azerbaijan. Built on the coast by the Caspian Sea, it's officially 28 metres below sea level with a famous medieval quarter.

The Naftalan Spa has been popular since the 6th century BC and bathing there in its crude oil is claimed to heal everything from impotence to skin problems.

Tea is the most popular drink in Azerbaijan. Traditionally served in a pear shaped glass, the drink is often consumed through lumps of sugar or jam, held in the mouth.

Seven Beauties is a competition where seven girls are given hooks and different coloured threads. The girls must crochet stockings and the winner is the girl who crochets the best in the shortest time.

Bread is considered sacred and something to share with friends. People will even kiss bread they find on the ground and sometimes hang it from a tree.

Azerbaijan is home to the first known fireplace and was also the site of the world's first oil well, just outside Baku.

Toyug kebabs

You will need

Kebabs: 1kg chicken thigh fillets, 1 tbs olive oil, 1 tbs lemon juice, ½ small chopped onion, pinch salt, pinch black pepper, pinch sugar.
Garnish: ½ red onion sliced in thin rings, 25g chopped coriander, 25g chopped parsley, ½ tsp sumac, lemon wedges.

Method

Cut chicken into bite size pieces and mix with olive oil, lemon juice, onion, salt, pepper and sugar in a glass or plastic bowl. Leave to marinate for at least 2 hours, preferably overnight.

Put chicken on skewers and grill or barbecue, then remove meat from skewers.

Sprinkle with coriander, parsley, sumac and onion, then season and serve with lemon wedges.

Yoghurt and herb soup

You will need

½ tbs olive oil, 1 chopped garlic clove, ½ chopped onion, 30g rice, 250ml chicken stock, 90g minced lamb or beef, 250g Greek yoghurt, ½ tbs plain flour, 1 small egg, beaten, 100g canned chickpeas, drained, Chopped mixed herbs (a small bunch of dill, a small bunch of coriander, a small bunch of mint, a small bunch of flat leaf parsley) 30g baby spinach, sliced, dried chilli flakes.

Method

Heat oil over medium heat. Add garlic and three quarters of the onion. Cook until translucent.

Add rice and cook until rice is lightly toasted.

Add stock and mix. Simmer for about 15 mins or until hte rice is tender.

Mix mince, the rest of the onion, salt and pepper and make into 2cm balls. Add to the simmering stock for 5 mins until cooked through. Transfer to a bowl.

Beat egg, add yoghurt and flour and whisk until smooth. Add half the stock and mix, then return to pan. Stir over medium heat for 8 mins until thick and simmering.

Add meatballs and chickpeas. Stir for 2 mins until heated through. Add herbs and spinach, and cook until wilted.

Season and serve scattered with chilli flakes.

> *"Finishing second means you are the first person to lose"*

Plov
(Lamb pilaf)

You will need

1tsb olive oil,
350g lamb leg, deboned and cut in bite-size pieces,
2 garlic cloves, 1 carrot, 1 onion,
1 tsp ground cumin, 50g dried apricots,
40g dried chestnuts, 125g rice, pinch of saffron,
125ml beef stock, some flat leaf parsley.

Method

Fry lamb pieces at high heat for 4 mins until well browned, Transfer to bowl.

Chop and add garlic, carrots and onions to pan and cook until golden. Add cumin. Chop and add the apricots and chestnuts, then add 170ml water. Bring to the boil, simmer for 1 hour until tender.

Meanwhile, soak rice in 250ml salted water for 30 minutes. Drain, then add saffron and transfer to saucepan.

Add stock and 2 tbs water. Cover and bring to the boil, then reduce heat to low and cook 10 mins.

Remove from heat and stand for 10 mins.

Spoon rice onto a plate and serve topped with lamb and parsley.

Badimjan dolmasi
(Stuffed aubergine)

You will need

4 medium aubergines, 300g minced lamb or beef,
1 large onion, finely chopped, salt and pepper,
1 bunch coriander, ½ bunch dill, ½ bunch mint,
2 large chopped tomatoes, plain yoghurt,
crushed garlic.

Method

Slice the aubergines lengthwise, most of the way through. Sprinkle salt inside and let stand 30 mins, then rinse out.

Mix the meat and onion, then cook over medium heat until well done. Add salt, pepper, chopped herbs and 1 tomato and mix. Add butter or oil if needed and leave to cool.

Preheat the oven to 180C/gas 4.

Open the slit on an aubergine and fill with stuffing. Repeat for the others and arrange side by side in an oven dish with tomato arranged around. Cover with foil and cook until tender.

Alternatively, cook in a saucepan. Arrange as above, cover and cook at low heat until just tender. Add water or stock if needed.

Serve with plain yogurt and crushed garlic.

> *"I'm such a bastard. I don't ever want to lose the feeling, or let anyone else experience it"*

Minced meat kebabs

You will need

500g minced lamb or beef, zest of 1 large lemon,
1 large onion, finely chopped, 1 tsp sumac,
pinch salt and black pepper to season,
1 tsp garlic powder, 1 tbs flat leaf parsley, chopped,
plain boiled rice or pitta bread,
Mixed salad (lettuce, cucumber, sliced onion, sliced tomato, flat leaf parsley)
Chilli sauce.

Method

Mix all the main ingredients in a bowl or food processor until well combined and smooth. Chill in refrigerator for 2 hours or overnight.

Divide into eight portions and roll each into a sausage around a skewer.

Either place under a very hot grill or on a BBQ and turn once or twice during cooking until well browned and cooked through.

Serve with salad and rice or pitta bread.

Badimjan borani (Vegetable stew)

You will need

1 onion, 1 green pepper, 2 aubergines,
2 tomatoes, 2 potatoes, 2 gloves garlic,
salt and pepper to taste, 3 tbs olive oil.
To serve: ½ bunch chopped coriander.

Method

Wash vegetables and herbs. Peel and chop vegetables into small cubes, but keep them separate.

Fry onion until light brown, then layer peppers, tomatoes, aubergine and potato on top.

Cover and simmer over low heat. When juices start to come out of the tomatoes, add salt, pepper and garlic and gently mix everything together.

Simmer until tender.

Sprinkle with coriander to serve.

Sumac

Mentioned in some of the above recipes, sumac is a deep reddish powder, made from dried berries.

These days, sumac is not too hard to find in supermarkets, but a passable substitute is coriander seed, freshly roasted and ground.

Canada

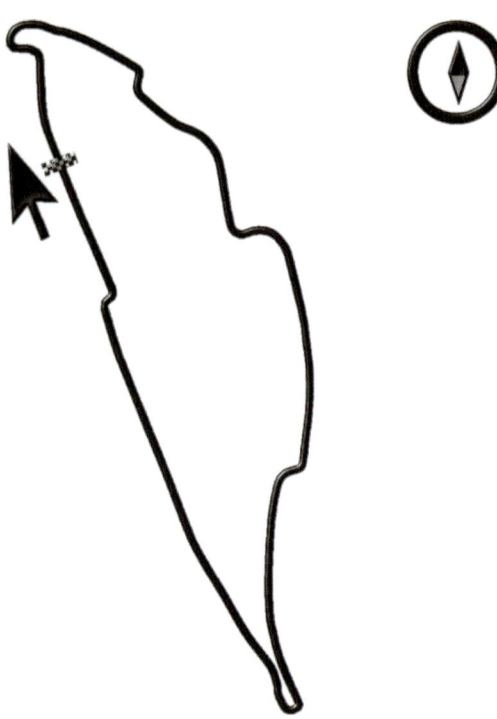

Circuit Gilles Villeneuve

Capacity	100,000
Length	4.361 Km (2.710 Miles)
Lap record	V Bottas (Mercedes) 2019 73.078 seconds

The circuit was built in 1978 on the man-made *Isle Notre Dame*, itself built in 1967.

It's probably best known for the infamous 'Wall of Champions' on the outside of the final turn. Touching it has ended the race for many a world champion over the years.

In the weeks before a Grand Prix, the city traps and removes as many groundhogs as possible around the course, but they have still caused many race day incidents.

Montreal

Montreal is the largest city in Quebec, set on an island in the Saint Lawrence River and named after Mount Royal, the three-peaked hill at its centre. It's one of the five largest French-speaking cities in the world.

Quebec is perhaps best known for poutine and smoked meat, but French-Canadian cooking also includes cretons, which is a paste made from finely minced pork, with cinnamon, savory, and cloves. It's popular spread on toast at breakfast.

Canadians are famously hospitable, so it's not surprising the first UFO Landing Platform was built in Alberta back in 1967. No alien visitors have used it so far, though.

Some things you should watch out for during a stay in Montreal: firstly, it is illegal to create, possess or sell crime comics, or to waterski after sunset.

It is also illegal to steal oysters or frighten the Queen. In Quebec City, it's also illegal to swear in French or to impersonate a foreigner.

Poutine
(Chips with gravy and cheese curds)

You will need

Oil for deep-frying,
500g potatoes, cut into thin chips,
250g coarse cottage cheese,
300ml beef gravy (can use granules),
black pepper.

Method

Prepare or heat the gravy, add ground black pepper to taste.

Get the oil hot, then fry chips (in batches if needed) until crisp. Drain and transfer to serving plate.

Crumble cottage cheese over the top, then pour on the gravy.

Variations

Add diced cooked chicken or hamburger.
Replace cottage cheese with other cheese.
Use light BBQ sauce instead of beef gravy.

Yellow split pea soup with ham

You will need

300g yellow split peas,
100g coarsely chopped ham, 2 carrots, ½ onion,
2-3 stalks celery, all diced.
1 tsp dried thyme, 1 bay leaf, 1 tbs salt,
pinch black pepper.

Method

Put split peas, ham, carrots, onion, celery, thyme, bay leaf, salt and pepper in a large pot with enough water to cover.

Boil and skim off any foam. Cover and simmer, stirring occasionally for about 3 hours until split peas are tender and soup thickens.

Easy bannock
(Quick bread)

You will need

280g flour, 4 tsp baking powder, ½ tsp salt, 120g butter or lard, 240ml milk, 240ml water, butter or lard for greasing oven dish.

Method

Preheat oven to 230C/gas 8. Grease a large oven dish and mix the dry ingredients in a bowl, rubbing in the butter or lard until a flaky texture is achieved.

Add milk and water and stir until you have a slightly lumpy batter. Pour batter into the oven dish and bake 20-25 mins until the middle is firm and springy.

> *"Honestly, what are we doing? Racing or ping-pong?"*

Canadian baked beans

You will need

400g can haricot beans, drained, 1 onion, chopped, 1 tsp mustard powder, 2 tsp black pepper, 200ml maple syrup, 150g thick cut smoked bacon, coarsely diced, salt.

Method

Preheat oven to 130C/gas ½.

Put beans, onion, mustard, pepper, salt, and maple syrup in a large pot. Add water to cover. Cover and bake 2-3 hours, adding water as needed.

Add bacon and bake another hour. Serve with brown bread.

Apple, potato and onion hash

You will need

2 large potatoes, 1 tbs olive oil, 2 tbs butter, 2 small apples, chopped, 1 small onion, chopped, salt and pepper.

Method

Prick potatoes with a fork and boil for 10 mins. Leave to cool, then dice them.

Heat oil and butter to medium heat and add apples and onions. Cook 5 mins. Add potatoes and season to taste.

Crisp and brown potatoes with apples and onions for another 5 mins, then serve.

Cheese spinach dip

You will need

225g cream cheese, 60ml mayonnaise, 50g grated Parmesan, 50g grated mature Cheddar, 1 garlic clove, ½ tsp dried basil, pinch garlic salt, 175g frozen chopped spinach, 50g grated mild Cheddar.

Method

Preheat oven to 180C/gas 4 and lightly grease a small baking dish.

Thaw and drain the spinach. Peel and finely chop the garlic.

Mix together cream cheese, mayonnaise, Parmesan, mature Cheddar, garlic, basil, garlic salt. Season to taste and stir in the spinach.

Transfer to the baking dish, top with the mild Cheddar and bake 25 mins until bubbly and lightly browned.

> *"Oh, the annoying octopus is back"*

Bacon and Cheddar flan

You will need

15g unsalted butter, plus some for greasing,
100g mushrooms, thinly sliced,
75g thick sliced smoked back bacon diced,
1 tbs chopped flat leaf parsley, ½ tsp black pepper,
6 eggs, 450ml double cream, ½ tsp salt,
½ tsp chilli powder, 80g mature Cheddar, grated.

Method

Preheat the oven to 180C/gas 4.

Butter a 15cm baking dish.

Melt butter in pan and cook mushrooms over moderate heat until liquid evaporates, then raise the heat to medium-high and stir-fry until browned.

Transfer to baking dish and add the bacon, parsley and pepper. Mix and spread in an even layer.

Whisk eggs well, add and whisk cream, salt and chilli, then pour over the mushrooms and bacon.

Sprinkle cheese over the top and bake until just set, about 50 mins. Transfer to rack and cool 15 mins.

Cut into squares and serve hot or warm.

Apple and tuna salad

You will need

Salad: 100g can tuna, 1 tbs lemon juice, 250g unpeeled diced red apple, 125g celery.

Dressing: 2 tbs mayonnaise, ½ tbs English mustard, ½ tbs honey, 1 tsp lemon juice.

Method

Mix dressing ingredients well and chill.

Sprinkle lemon juice over apples. Drain and flake tuna.

Mix everything together and serve.

France

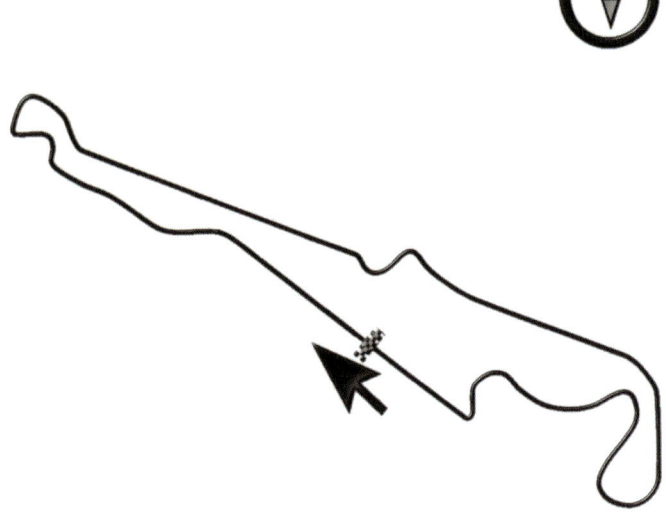

Circuit Paul Ricard

Capacity	90,000
Length	5.861 Km (3.642 Miles)
Lap record	S Vettel (Ferrari) 2019
	92.740 seconds

The track is characterised by the very long Mistral straight and a lack of changes in height, since it is built on a plateau.

The track is also known for it's distinctive runoff areas, the Blue Zone and Red Zone, designed to minimise braking distance at the expense of extreme tyre wear.

This year's race will be the first F1 Grand Prix at Circuit Paul Ricard since 1990.

Le Castellet

Le Castellet is a medieval village, situated in the Var department of the Provence-Alpes-Côte d'Azur region, south east France. It is 8km north of the beaches of Bandol and 20km north-west of Toulon, next to La Cadière-d'Azur and Le Beausset.

Note that the French consider a positive attitude to be a bad thing and that ignoring negatives is naïve. Apparently, the French view is that seeing the defects first is a sign of competence and intelligence.

Also note that no person may name their pig Napoleon, and every French citizen must have a haystack, in case the king passes by with his horse.

Unless a woman is holding the reigns of a horse or riding a bike, she is not allowed to wear trousers. And it is illegal to kiss on or at a railway station or train.

Finally, please remember that no alcohol whatsoever is allowed in a place of work – presumably including those parts of a race track used by the teams – except for beer, wine, cidre and poiré. Seems fair enough.

French onion soup

You will need

50g butter, 750g onions, 2 tsp sugar,
2 tsp plain flour, 1l beef stock, salt, black pepper,
crusty French bread, grated cheese.

Method
Melt butter, and add thinly sliced onions.
Cook on low heat until even, dark brown. This should take 20-30 mins.
Add flour and stir for 5 mins. Add stock, salt and ground black pepper to taste. Simmer 15-20 mins.

Slice bread 2cm thick and toast one side. Turn and cover with grated cheese, then toast until golden.

Pour soup into a bowl and lay cheesy toast on top. Repeat with rest of soup and toast.

Courgettes with prawns

You will need
4 medium courgettes, 25g butter,
1 onion, finely chopped,
150g canned chopped tomatoes,
75g prawns, chopped, 1-2 tbs breadcrumbs,
chilli sauce, lemon juice, 2 tbs grated Parmesan,
salt and black pepper.

Method
Boil courgettes for 5 mins in salted water. Drain and run under cold water. Melt butter and add onion and cook until transparent and soft.

Halve the courgettes lengthwise and scoop out flesh with a teaspoon. Chop and mix with onion, tomatoes and prawns. Add breadcrumbs to create a fairly dry mixture, then season with salt and pepper and add chilli sauce and lemon juice to taste.

Put the mixture back in the courgette shells and sprinkle with Parmesan.

Bake in a buttered dish for 20 mins until cheese is lightly browned.

Plaice with grapefruit

You will need
125g potatoes, 375g plaice fillets,
1tbs plain flour, 25g butter, 75ml grapefriut juice,
1egg yolk, ½ tsp sugar, salt, pepper.

Method

Peel potatoes, boil or steam until tender, adding seasoning. Slice and keep hot.

Coat each plaice fillet well with seasoned flour. Fry in butter 1-2 mins each side.
Pour over grapefruit juice, cover and cook for 5 mins. Place on serving dish.

Beat egg yolk with sugar and 1 tbs water in a bowl. Place over pan of hot water and beat until it thickens a little. Season.

Pour sauce over fish and serve hot with the potatoes.

"If this thing comes off what happens?"

Boeuf Bourguignon
(Beef in a red wine sauce)

You will need

1 tbs olive oil, 170g bacon, roughly chopped,
1½ kg beef brisket, trimmed of fat, in 5cm chunks,
1 large carrot in 1cm slices, 1 large onion, diced,
6 cloves garlic, minced, salt, pepper, 2 tbs flour,
12 baby onions (optional), 700ml red wine,
500ml beef stock, 2 tbs tomato puree,
1 beef stock cube, crushed,
1 tsp fresh thyme, finely chopped,
2 tbs fresh parsley, finely chopped,
2 bay leaves, 500g small mushrooms, quartered,
2 tbs butter

Method

In a large, heavy based pot at medium heat, fry bacon in 1 tbs oil until crisp and brown. Transfer with a slotted spoon to a large dish and set aside.

Pat beef dry with a paper towel, then fry in batches in the same oil until evenly browned. Remove and add to the dish with the bacon.

In the same oil, fry the carrots and diced onions until softened, (about 3 minutes), then add 2/3 of the minced garlic and cook for 1 minute. Drain off excess fat and return the bacon and beef to the pot. Season with salt and pepper. Sprinkle with flour, toss well to coat and cook to brown well.

Add baby onions, wine and enough stock to barely vcover the meat. Add the tomato puree, stock cube and herbs. Bring to a boil, then cover and simmer for 1½ to 2 hours, stirring occasionally, until the meat is falling apart.

Fry rest of garlic in butter for 5 mins, shaking the pan occasionally to coat with butter. Season with salt and pepper.

Mushrooms to the pot and simmer 5 mins, stirring occasionally. Garnish with parsley and serve with mashed potatoes, rice or noodles.

Pork chops in orange sauce

You will need

25g butter, 4 large pork chops, rind removed, 150ml orange juice, pinch chopped or dried thyme, salt, pepper.

To serve: 1 orange, thinly sliced, 2 tbs chopped parsley.

Method
Fry chops in butter, turning, until cooked. Remove and keep warm. Add orange juice to pan. Stir to mix with meat juices. Bring to boil, then simmer to reduce by half. Season with salt, pepper and thyme.

Pour sauce over chops. Garnish with orange slices and sprinkle with chopped parsley.

Salmon in foil

You will need
4 salmon steaks, olive oil, 2 tbs lemon juice, 2 tbs chopped fresh herbs, 50g butter, salt and pepper, baking foil.

Method
Descale salmon, wash and pat dry.

Lightly oil 4 pieces of baking foil and wrap each around a piece of salmon, sprinkled with lemon and herbs. Add a knob of butter and season.

Seal packets. Bake at 200C/gas 6 for 20-25 mins.

> "Don't shout, f*****.
> When I have a chance, but not in
> the middle of the fast corners"

Provençale salad

You will need

1 medium onion, sliced into thin rings,
1 tsp caster sugar, 1 tbs wine vinegar,
8 anchovy fillets, ½ crisp lettuce, shredded,
3 tomatoes, skinned and quartered,
100g cooked French beans, halved,
50g black olives,
1 small red or green pepper, diced, ¼ cucumber, thinly sliced,
3 hard-boiled eggs, quartered.

Dressing: 2 garlic cloves, 4 tbs olive oil,
2 tbs lemon juice, 2 tbs tomato puree, salt, pepper.

Method

Marinate the onion with the sugar and vinegar in a bowl for 30 mins.

Put lettuce in a bowl, add the quartered tomatoes, beans, olives, pepper, cucumber and anchovies and toss to mix.

Drain onion rings, reserving vinegar. Put garlic, oil, lemon juice, vinegar from onions and tomato puree in a blender, blend and season to taste.

Pour dressing over salad, arrange egg quarters and onion rings on top.

Merguez
(Spicy lamb sausages)

You will need

Seeds: 1 tsp cumin, 1 tsp fennel, 1 tsp coriander.
Powders: 1 tbs paprika, 1 tsp cayenne or chilli, ¼ tsp cinnamon.
500g minced lamb,
40ml olive oil, 25g chopped coriander,
10g chopped mint, 2 cloves garlic, finely chopped,
1 tsp salt.

Method

Dry roast seeds over medium heat for 2 mins until fragrant. Allow to cool, then grind finely.

Add paprika, cayenne and cinnamon. Put lamb in a bowl, drizzle with oil and sprinkle with spice mix.

Add herbs, garlic and salt and mix well. Let stand an hour or two.

Form into sausage shapes and chill before using. These can be made in advance and refrigerated for a few days.

Fry until cooked right through. Serve stuffed into a bread bun or pitta or serve in Middle Eastern flatbreads with fresh salad.

---

*"Unbelievable! I have no idea what just happened.
Someone just pushed me"*

Austria

Red Bull Ring

Capacity	40,000
Length	4.318 Km (2.683 Miles)
Lap record	C Sainz (McLaren) 2020 65.619 seconds

In 2011, Red Bull became the owner of the Österreichring at Spielberg, and the Austrian Grand Prix returned to the F1 calendar in 2014 after a ten year gap.

Most of the original high-speed bends were replaced when the track was redesigned by Hermann Tilke in 1997. More recently, the exit of turn one was changed to discourage drivers running wide to gain an advantage, and the same has been done at turn eight.

Spielberg

The city of Spielberg, with a population of about 5,000, is located north of the river Mur, between the cities of Zeltweg and Knittelfeld, a little to the south of central Austria.

When the Turks fled from Vienna in 1683, they left coffee beans, launching the great Viennese Kaffeehaus tradition.

The Austrian Kipferl, similar to a croissant, features in Viennese legend which claims it mimics the battle flags of the Ottomans and celebrates victory over the Turks.

Before drinking, Austrians toast by clinking glasses and looking the other person in the eye. Not making eye contact is considered rude and also bad luck, bringing upon oneself seven years of bad sex.

The Tracht traditional folk costume is accepted in Austria as formal wear and can even be worn to the Viennese Opera. Men wear green Loden jackets and Lederhosen and women wear Dirndl dresses.

Wiener schnitzel
(Meat cutlets)

You will need

4 thin veal fillets, 150-180g each
(or use pork, chicken or turkey)
2 eggs, 100g flour,
100g breadcrumbs,
salt, pepper, clarified butter or oil, sliced lemon, to garnish.

Method

Beat the meat until thin and season both sides. Put flour and breadcrumbs on separate plates, beat eggs and put them on another plate.

Coat each piece of meat in flour onboth sides, draw through the beaten eggs to coat evenly, then coat in breadcrumbs, pressing them down with the back of a fork.

Heat enough butter or oil in a large pan for the coated meat pieces to float. When the fat is hot enough to hiss when breadcrumbs are added, add meat pieces and fry for 2-4 minutes until golden. Carefully turn using a spatula and fry the other side to match.

Drain and set aside on kitchen paper, then arrange on a plate and garnish with lemon.

Serve with potato salad or mixed salad.

Austrian potato salad

You will need

500g waxy potatoes, peeled and cut in 1cm slices,
125ml vegetable stock, 125ml water,
pinch salt, ½ tbs sugar, 15ml white vinegar,
½ tbs Dijon mustard, 30ml oil, 1 small red onion,
3 cornichons or small gherkins,
15g chopped chives, pinch black pepper.

Method

Boil potatoes in stock, water, salt, sugar, and ½ tbs vinegar. Reduce heat to medium-low, cover, and cook until tender. Remove cover, and cook on high heat for 2 minutes.

Drain potatoes, reserving 1 tbs of liquid. Whisk the retained liquid with the remaining vinegar, mustard and oil.

Put about half the potatoes in a bowl with the cooking liquid mixture and mash until a thick sauce forms. Add remaining potatoes, onion, cornichons, and chives and combine gently.

Season and serve warm or cold.

"I should have known really that he's mental..."

Tiroler gröstl
(Alpine bacon, onion and potato)

You will need

1½ tbs oil, 400g smoked bacon lardons,
1 onion, coarsely chopped,
500g boiled waxy potatoes in small chunks,
1 tsp caraway seeds, 1 tsp paprika,
½ tsp chilli powder (optional),
1 tbs chopped parsley, 1 egg.

Method

Heat oil and fry bacon and onion until the bacon is golden. Transfer to plate, then fry the potatoes until golden.

Tip in the caraway, paprika and chilli and season, then fry for another minute.

Return the bacon and onion, taste for seasoning, then add the parsley. Transfer to plate. Fry egg and serve on top.

Cod baked in foil

You will need

4 pieces thick cod fillet, 700-900g in total,
60ml olive oil, 1 tsp minced garlic,
4 tbs chopped parsley or basil,
lemon to garnish, salt and pepper to taste.

Method

Preheat baking dish in oven at 200C/gas 6, then take 8 pieces of foil, each about 50cm long, using them in pairs to make 4 packages.

Rub a piece of fish with oil, season and place on foil. Sprinkle with garlic and herbs, then fold, crimping the edges tight. Repeat with rest of fish pieces.

Place the packets in the baking dish and bake about 15 minutes. Rest for a couple of minutes, then open the package. Spoon out fish and serve with lemon.

Option: Mix 1 diced plum tomato, some black olives, capers and thinly sliced onion and add inside the packets before baking.

---

*"We need to get it up.
I wish I could still get it up"*

Bacon onion spätzle
(Bacon and onion with pasta drops)

You will need

500g plain flour, pinch salt, pinch nutmeg,
3 eggs, lightly beaten, 250ml milk,
120g smoked bacon, diced, 1 onion, chopped,
1 tbs olive oil, chopped fresh parsley.

Method

Sieve flour into a bowl. Make a well in the centre and add the eggs and milk gradually, whisking until a smooth batter is formed. Let stand 30 minutes.

Press batter through a sieve into boiling salted water and cook 1 minute, then drop cooked spätzle into iced water. Drain and set aside.

Cook the bacon in a pan over medium heat for 4 to 5 minutes. Add onions and cook until soft. In a separate pan, lightly fry the cooked spätzle until golden, then add the bacon mixture, seasoning as needed with salt and pepper. Garnish with parsley.

Tomaten kohl
(Fried tomato and cabbage)

You will need

500g savoy cabbage, 1 tbs lard,
125g chopped onions, 400g diced tomatoes,
400g passata, ½ tbs cider vinegar,
½ tsp salt, 1 tsp white pepper,
1 tsp caraway seeds, ½ tsp allspice.

Method

Melt lard in a large pan and add onions. Fry at low heat until translucent. Cut cabbage in approx. 2x5cm strips and add to pan, stirring to mix.

Sprinkle vinegar over cabbage, then add salt, pepper, and caraway seeds. Simmer about 10 minutes, stirring occasionally. Add tomatoes and passata.

Stir in allspice and season to taste. Cover and simmer 30-40 minutes.

"What is he doing? Hey! Someone tell him to get a steering wheel!"

Great Britain

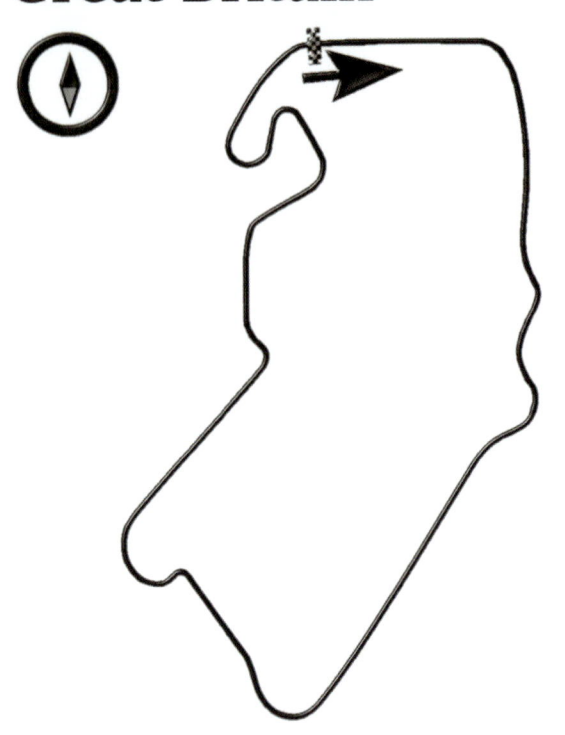

Silverstone Circuit

Capacity	150,000
Length	5.891 Km (3.661 Miles)
Lap record	L Hamilton (Mercedes) 2017 87.369 seconds

Silverstone hosted the first round of what became the F1 world championship in 1950, and all those since 1987.

Less than half of those who started on pole have gone on to win the British Grand Prix.

Maggotts corner is the fastest of any circuit in the world, with cars driving through at up to 180mph, pulling in excess of 4.5g. About 66% of the lap is at full throttle.

Silverstone

Silverstone village, 6.4 km from Towcester, has a population of 2,176. In the Middle Ages, the village primarily traded in timber, a tradition which continues to this day.

10,000 litres of tomato sauce will be used in the catering wagons around the circuit, and it's estimated 20,000 bottles of mineral water, 10,000 bottles of wine and 6,000 bottles of champagne are consumed during a typical Silverstone F1 race weekend.

The British also consume 97% of the world's baked beans. So it's probably best not to share a tent.

Great Britain has also produced more F1 drivers than any other nation – 144, out of a total of 695, so far.

A defrocked priest named Cornelius Horan was jailed for two months after running across the Hangar Straight, mid-race, in 2003. He wore a kilt and carried a banner with the words 'Read the Bible'.

Scotch eggs

You will need

6 eggs, 400g sausage meat,
2 tbs curly parsley, finely chopped,
2 tsp brown sauce, 2 tsp mustard powder,
1 tsp ground mace,
4 rashers smoked streaky bacon,
45g plain flour, 100g breadcrumbs.

Method

Boil 4 of the eggs for 5 mins, then plunge them into cold water.

Mix sausage meat, parsley, brown sauce, mustard and mace. Season. Add 1 beaten egg and mix. Divide into four portions.

Beat remaining egg and pour onto a plate. Put seasoned flour on another plate. Spread breadcrumbs on a third plate.

Drop bacon into boiling water for a few moments, then remove and drain.

Peel the boiled eggs. Wrap each with a slice of bacon. Roll in flour and shake off excess. Mould sausage meat around it, then dip in the beaten egg and roll in breadcrumbs. Cover and chill for 4 hrs or overnight.

When ready to eat, heat a deep frying pan medium hot and carefully lower in eggs 2-3 at a time. Fry for about 5 mins, turning until golden. Serve hot or cold.

Cornish pasties

You will need

Pastry: Make the alternative pastry as directed in Appendix 1, page 90.
Filling: 200g finely diced potato,
75g finely diced swede, 75g finely chopped onion,
200g minced beef, ½ tbs plain flour, 20g butter,
1 small beaten egg.

Method

Pastry: Roll out the dough and cut into 6 circles, using a dinner plate as a template.

Preheat oven to 180C/gas 4.

Filling: Season vegetables. Mix beef with flour and season. Spoon potatoes, swede, onions and beef on one half of a circle, leaving a gap round the edge. Dot with butter and brush around edges with beaten egg. Fold pastry over and crimp to seal.

Brush with beaten egg and make a steam hole in the centre with a sharp knife.

Repeat for the other pasties. Bake 50 mins until crispy and golden. Cool 5-10 mins.

*"That's hot air.
It's blowing hot air at me!"*

Roast beef with caramelised onion gravy

You will need

½ tbs black peppercorns, ½ tbs mustard powder, ½ tsp dried thyme, ½ tsp celery seeds, ½ tbs olive oil, about 700g beef roasting joint, 1 tbs plain flour, 1 beef stock cube, 1 tbs onion chutney or marmalade, 1 tsp Marmite, salt.

Method – see Yorkshire pudding recipe!
Grind peppercorns, mustard, thyme and celery seeds with a little salt. Stir in oil, then rub mixture all over the beef. Ideally, cover and chill overnight.

Preheat oven to 190C/gas 5. Lay beef in a roasting tin. Roast 25-30 mins per 500g plus an extra 25-30 mins.

Remove from oven, cover with foil and rest 30 mins. If making the Yorkshire puddings, increase oven to 220C/gas 7.

For gravy, pour juices from roasting tin into a jug. Let separate, then spoon 1 tbs fat back to the tin (or use butter). With the tin on the hob, stir in flour, stock cubes, onion chutney and Marmite. Cook for 1 min, stirring to scrape up any meat bits in tin.

Gradually stir in 200ml hot water and keep stirring while it thickens, then keep warm.
Slice the beef. Drizzle with gravy to serve.

Yorkshire puddings

You will need
450ml milk, 4 large eggs, 250g plain flour, 2 tbs oil, salt.

Method

Blend or whisk milk, eggs, flour and 2 tsp salt to a smooth batter. Cover and leave for at least 15 mins, ideally approx. 2 hours.

With oven at 220C/gas 7, brush 12 holes of a muffin tin with oil. Heat tin in oven for 5 mins, then lift out and quickly pour batter into the holes.

Bake 5 mins, then reduce oven to 200C/gas 6 and cook 30 mins until puffed, risen and golden.

Note

If serving with the roast beef, prepare the batter before putting the beef in the oven, so the batter has time to stand. Then, cook Yorkshire puddings while the gravy is being prepared.

> *"In sport, there is never any moment that is the same as the other"*

Bubble and squeak cakes

You will need

½ small cauliflower in small florets,
500g potatoes in 25mm dice,
1 carrot cut into 10mm dice,
1 parsnip cut into 10mm dice, 1
 tbs butter, salt, pepper,
4 strips thick cut bacon, cut into 15mm strips,
250g Brussels sprouts, shredded, 4 tbs oil,
6 eggs, 1 tbs chopped chives.

Method

Simmer potatoes, cauliflower, carrots and parsnips in salted water until just tender. Drain well, transfer to bowl with butter, season and very roughly mash.

Fry bacon over medium heat until brown. Remove from pan and mix with vegetables leaving as much fat in the pan as you can.

Fry sprouts over medium heat until tender, mix with the vegetables and divide into 6 even patties. Refrigerate until needed.

Fry the patties in batches until the bottoms turn golden brown, then flip and repeat until evenly browned.

Heat oil in non-stick pan to medium heat. Break 3 eggs into pan, season and fry until whites are set. Place 1 egg on top of each bubble and squeak cake. Repeat with remaining eggs. Serve topped with chives.

Ploughman's lunch

You will need

Variety of hard cheeses, such as Cheddar, Stilton, Cheshire, Red Leicester, sliced ham,
sliced cured meats,
pickles of your choice, such as chunky brown pickle, onions, beetroot, mustard, dill,
English mustard, butter, apple wedges,
hard-boiled eggs,
bread, white or wholemeal.

Method

Simply arrange a selection of the ingredients on a platter or in a basket.

Be sure to include some of each of the different types of meats, cheeses, pickles, apple, egg and buttered bread.

Serve with a pint of cold beer – ideally a good English pale ale or bitter.

"I am losing one second a lap because of the options. One second!"

Hungary

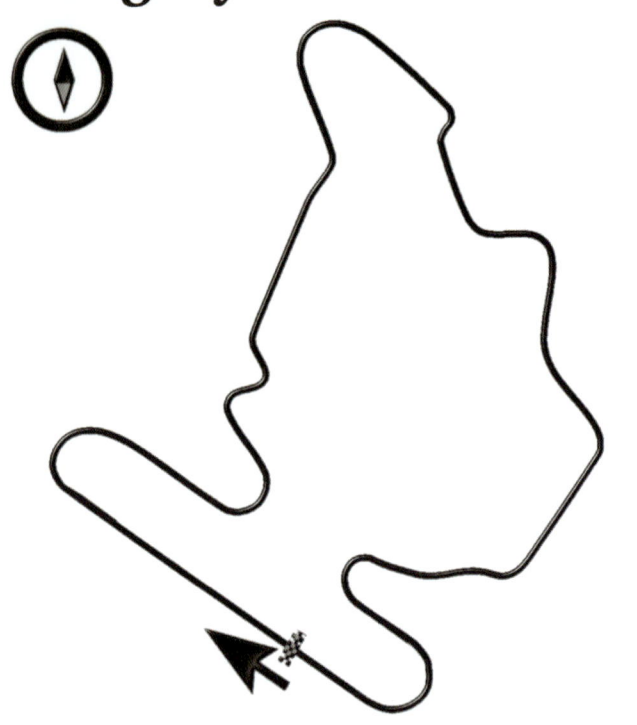

Hungaroring

Capacity	70,000
Length	4.381 Km (2.722 Miles)
Lap record	M Verstappen (Red Bull) 2019 77.103 seconds

The Hungaroring is normally dusty due to under-use throughout most of the year and its sandy soil. Despite this, it often becomes faster during qualifying, so teams try to set qualifying laps as late as possible.

As it's such a twisty, bumpy track, it is also compared in style to Monaco. Overtaking is difficult, making qualifying well vital.

Budapest

The Hungaroring is outside the town of Mogyoród. The original idea was for a street circuit similar to Monaco to be built within Budapest's largest park, but the government decided to build it 18km away from the city, close to a major highway.

There are more than 500 thermal springs in Hungary, including about 150 spas, so there's no excuse not to take a bath!

The famous Rubik's Cube was invented by Hungarian engineer, Ernö Rubik. It's almost as twisty as the Hungaroring itself...

Apparently, Budapest's Vajdahunyad Castle was originally built of cardboard and wood. When it proved popular, it was rebuilt in stone.

No meal is complete without adding hot chilli sauce or ground hot or sweet paprika, and any dish simply has to be smothered in tejföl – sour cream.

(You'll find a recipe for a hot chilli-garlic sauce in the appendix).

Fisherman's soup

You will need

800g perch or sea bass,
2 tbs olive oil,
1 onion, finely chopped,
1 small green pepper, finely chopped,
600g (1½ cans) tomatoes, coarsely mashed,
1 tbs sweet paprika,
sour cream, chopped parsley.

Method

Cut body of fish into 3cm pieces and chill.

Fry fish heads and bones in 1 tbs oil for 2 mins. Add 1½ litres water and simmer 30 mins. Strain through sieve, keep liquid and discard solids.

Fry onions and pepper over medium heat 4 mins until softened. Add tomatoes and cook 5 mins. Add paprika and stir-fry 1 min until fragrant. Return strained stock to pan.

Simmer 40 mins and season to taste. Add fish pieces, simmer 10 mins until just cooked. Check seasoning again.

Serve in bowls, topped with sour cream and parsley. Serve with crusty bread.

Rakott krumpli
(Baked potato, sausage and egg)

You will need

1kg waxy potatoes,
1 tsp oil, 200g spicy smoked sausages, sliced,
60g butter (plus extra for greasing),
8 hard-boiled eggs, sliced, 600ml sour cream,
35g dry breadcrumbs.

Method

Preheat oven to 200C/gas 6.

Put potatoes in salted water. Bring to boil, then simmer on low heat until just tender. Drain, cool, peel and thickly slice.

Fry sausage slices over high heat 2 mins until light golden. Drain on paper towel.

Grease a deep 40cm baking dish with butter. Add a third of the potatoes, top with half the eggs and half the sausages.

Season to taste and spoon about a third of the sour cream over the top.

Repeat with another layer of potatoes, eggs and sausages and finish with a final layer of potatoes. Season and add remaining sour cream.

Sprinkle with breadcrumbs and drizzle with melted butter. Bake 30 mins until golden.

"I will drive flat out all the time, I love racing"

Cucumber salad

You will need

1 long, thin cucumber, peeled and thinly sliced,
1 tsp salt, ½ tsp caster sugar,
2 tbs white wine vinegar, 1 garlic clove, crushed,
2 tsp paprika, 75 ml water.

Method

Mix cucumber thoroughly with salt, then set aside 1 hour or until softened.

Squeeze out any excess liquid, place in a colander and rinse under running water. Drain and transfer to a bowl.

Mix sugar, vinegar, garlic, paprika and water and stir until sugar dissolves. Pour over cucumbers and season well.

Refrigerate for 2 hours before serving.

Goulash

You will need

350g diced beef or steak, olive oil,
1 small onion, coarsely chopped,
1 small red pepper, chopped into medium pieces,
1 bay leaf, 1 tbs tomato puree, 1 tbs paprika,
salt and pepper to taste.

Method

Fry beef in oil in a large saucepan. Drain juices and keep to one side. When meat is browned, add onion and peppers and fry until soft.

Add reserved cooking juices, bay leaf, tomato puree and paprika and stir.

Cook for about 1 hour until tender.

Add water and season.

Lettuce and smoky bacon salad

You will need

Leaves from 1 iceberg lettuce,
1 tsp caster sugar,
1 tbs white wine vinegar,
100g smoked bacon lardons.

Method

Fry lardons until golden brown.

Pour boiling water over leaves in a colander until they start to wilt. Refresh under cold running water. Drain and transfer to bowl.

Mix sugar, vinegar and 2 tbs water until sugar dissolves. Pour over lettuce and toss with lardons. Refrigerate before serving.

"He's just a total bloody idiot. Always was, always will be"

Pörkölt with nokedli
(Meat casserole with pasta drops)

You will need

Pörkölt: 1 small onion, finely chopped,
2 tbs oil, 1 tsp paprika, 50ml beef stock,
350g diced beef or steak, ½ tsp salt,
1 garlic clove, crushed, ½ tsp chilli powder,
1 mild chilli, chopped, 1 tomato, chopped.
Nokedli: ½ tsp salt, 1 egg, 150ml water,
200g plain flour, butter or oil.

Method

Pörkölt: Fry onion until golden. Remove from heat. Stir in paprika and chilli powder.
Add stock and simmer to reduce slightly. Add meat, salt and garlic, stir well and simmer until meat is half cooked, about 30-60 mins depending on meat. Add mild chillies and tomato and cook until meat is tender. Season to tste.

Nokedli: Beat eggs with a little water. Sift flour and a pinch of salt into a bowl, then gently mix in the egg and rest of the water.

Boil a large pot of water, add the salt.
Push the dough through a colander into the boiling water and cook until the pieces rise to the surface. Remove with slotted spoon and toss in butter or oil.

Serve the Pörkölt on a bed of nokedli with cucumber salad.

Lángos
(Deep-fried potato flatbread)

You will need

1 large potato, boiled, peeled, mashed, kept warm,
2½ tsp instant yeast, 1 tsp sugar,
400g plain flour, 1 tbs oil, 1 tsp salt,
120ml milk, 2 cloves garlic, halved.
Optionally: sour cream, grated cheese.

Method

Mix freshly mashed potatoes, yeast, sugar, flour, oil, salt and milk thoroughly to form a kneadable dough. Knead until smooth and elastic. Cover until doubled in size.

Divide dough into 4 balls and place on a lightly floured board. Rest 20 mins.

Flatten and stretch each ball into a 20cm disc. Make 1 or more slits in the centre of each disc.

Fry discs one at a time, about 2 mins each side until golden. Drain on paper towels.

Serve hot, rubbed with garlic clove and sprinkled with salt.

Optionally, top with sour cream and/or grated mild Cheddar or Emmental.

Belgium

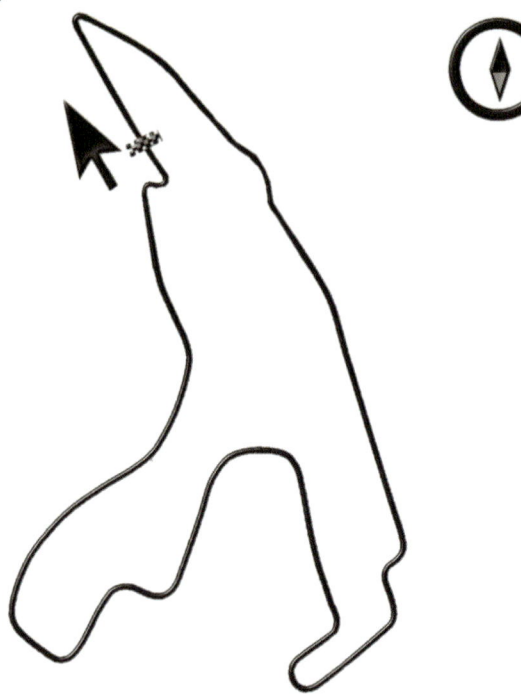

Circuit de Spa-Francorchamps

Capacity   70,000
Length   7.004 Km (4.352 Miles)
Lap record   V Bottas (Mercedes) 2018
              106.286 seconds

Spa emphasises driver skill more than any other track, especially the corners at Eau Rouge and Blanchimont. These have to be taken flat out to make the most of the following straights.

The circuit is also known for unpredictable weather, with wet and dry conditions often experienced at the same time, on different parts of the track.

Spa-Francorchamps

Francorchamps is part of the Stavelot municipality, a Walloon town near Liège.

Bread and potatoes are the traditional food staples in Belgium. Many meals include beef, chicken, and pork, while seafood is popular in the north. Popular drinks are beer and wine. Cooking is traditionally done with butter and there is high overall consumption of dairy products.

A Belgian law restricts 'games of chance', so prohibitions apply to commercial contests, sweepstakes, lotteries organised by advertisers and even private poker and bingo games, unless a licence is obtained.

Belgium has historically had a strict stance towards drugs, but personal possession of up to 3g of cannabis was legalised in 2003.
Another law says that horses, oxen, dogs, etc. may be requisitioned to draw army vehicles. 'Lift and coast' indeed.

Until recently, foreigners living in Belgium were forbidden to own pigeons, unless special permission was obtained from the Minister of Justice.

Carbonade flamande or stooflees
(Traditional Flemish stew)

You will need

400g beef, 2 onions, 1 medium carrot,
10g butter, 1 tbs plain flour, 1 tbs red wine vinegar,
250ml lager, 1 tbs brown sugar, 1 bay leaf,
1 tsp dried thyme, 1 cloves, 40g gingerbread,
sliced, salt, pepper.

Method

Cut meat in thick slices. Peel and slice the onions and carrots.

In a casserole, brown meat in butter, then season, add flour, onions and carrots. Mix well and cook for 5 mins to soften onions without colouring. Add vinegar and cook for a further 2 mins.

Add lager, 50 ml water, sugar, thyme, bay leaf, cloves and ⅔ of the gingerbread, cut into pieces.

Bring to boil. Cover and simmer 90 mins. Remove lid, increase heat and stir until the volume of liquid has reduced by about half.

Grill the remaining gingerbread slices and cut into cubes.

Serve the carbonade with Flemish frites and grilled gingerbread cubes.

Sole meunière
(Sole fried in seasoned flour)

You will need

120g plain flour, salt, black pepper,
4 fresh sole fillets, 75-100g each,
6 tbs butter, 1 tsp grated lemon zest,
6 tbs lemon juice, 1 tbs chopped fresh parsley.

Method

Preheat oven to low and warm plates.

Mix flour, 2 tsp salt and 1 tsp pepper on a plate. Rinse sole fillets. Pat dry with paper towels and sprinkle one side with salt.

Heat 3 tbs butter over medium heat until it starts to brown. Dredge sole fillets in flour both sides and put them in the hot butter.

Lower heat to medium-low, cook 2 mins on each side, turning carefully with a spatula.

While the second side cooks, add a large pinch of lemon zest and 3 tbs lemon juice to the pan. Transfer fillets to warmed plates and pour the sauce over them.

Repeat with the remaining fillets.

Sprinkle all the fillets with parsley, salt, and pepper and serve immediately.

> *"I'm going to pee in your seat!"*

Ham and endive gratin

You will need

1 tbs butter, 1 tbs plain flour,
220ml milk, salt, pepper,
2 endives, halved, 4 thin slices smoked ham,
100g grated Gruyere or mild Cheddar.

Method

Preheat oven to 180C/gas 4. Melt butter over medium heat. Whisk in flour. Cook for 1 min.

Whisk in milk. Cook for 5 mins at medium heat.

Season. Wrap endives in ham. Pour half of sauce into a baking dish, lay endives on top and pour over remaining sauce. Top with cheese, cover with foil and bake 25 mins. Remove foil. Bake 30 mins.

Stoemp

You will need

5 potatoes, peeled, 60g butter,
175ml single cream, 1 small onion, finely chopped,
2 garlic cloves, finely chopped,
4 medium leeks, finely sliced,
120ml vegetable stock, salt and pepper.

Method

Cook potatoes until tender, drain and mash.

Fry garlic and onion in butter until soft. Add leeks and fry until translucent. Add cream and stock.

Simmer 10 mins but do not boil.

Remove onions and reduce liquid by half. Mix onions with potatoes, return to the pan and stir well. Season to taste.

Belgian carrots

You will need

8 carrots, sliced across in 8mm pieces,
80ml double cream, 30g butter,
2 tsp sugar, 2 tsp dried parsley,
pinch nutmeg, salt, pepper.

Method

Put carrots in a medium saucepan, cover with water and simmer 10-12 mins until tender.

Drain carrots and toss them with the remaining ingredients. Stir over low heat until sauce is heated through.

Waterzooi
(Simple Belgian stew)

You will need

1 tbs oil, 500g chicken pieces,
1 sliced leek, 1 small onion, diced,
1 stalk celery, sliced,
1tsp salt, 600ml water,
1 chicken stock cube, pinch nutmeg,
2 tsp plain flour, 2 tsp lemon juice,
60ml double cream, 1 egg yolk,
1 tsp dried parsley.

Method

Heat oil in large pan over medium heat. Brown chicken. Drain and set aside.

Fry leeks, onion, celery and salt until tender. Return chicken to pot and add water, stock and nutmeg.

Simmer 35-40 mins until tender. Mix flour and lemon juice. Pour into pot and stir. Beat cream and egg with 1 tbs of stock and add to pot.

Heat through, but do not boil. Sprinkle with parsley to serve.

Liège salad
(Bacon, potato and bean salad)

You will need

500g potatoes,
500g green beans, in 75mm pieces,
250g thick cut bacon, diced, 1½ small onions, sliced, 120ml balsamic vinegar, salt, pepper to taste.

Method

Boil potatoes until tender, about 10 mins. Boil green beans about 5 mins in a separate pan. Drain.

Fry bacon over medium heat until crisp.

Remove and set aside. Fry onions in bacon fat until browned. Remove and set aside.

Pour balsamic vinegar into pan and stir to mix with the browned residue from pan.

In a large bowl, mix green beans, potatoes, onions and bacon. Pour the vinegar over and toss to coat. Season with salt and pepper.

Flemish frites

You will need

120ml mayonnaise, 1 tbs tomato puree,
1 tbs chopped red onion,
1 tsp finely chopped green pepper,
1 tsp finely chopped red pepper,
2 tsp lemon juice, pinch salt,
750g potatoes, oil for deep-frying.

Method

Mix mayonnaise, tomato puree, red onion, green pepper, red pepper, lemon juice and salt in bowl. Cover and refrigerate 8 hours.

Cut potatoes into chips and submerge in ice water. Rinse in cold water until clear. Drain and pat dry.

Heat oil in a deep-fryer or large saucepan to 150C, medium hot.

Fry potatoes in batches until cooked through but still white, about 5 mins. Drain and leave to cool to room temperature.

Heat oil to 190C, almost smoking. Fry chips again until deep golden, 5-10 mins.

Transfer chips to a paper-towel lined plate to drain. Season with salt and serve with the sauce.

"And that is Ralf Schumacher, son of Michael"

Netherlands

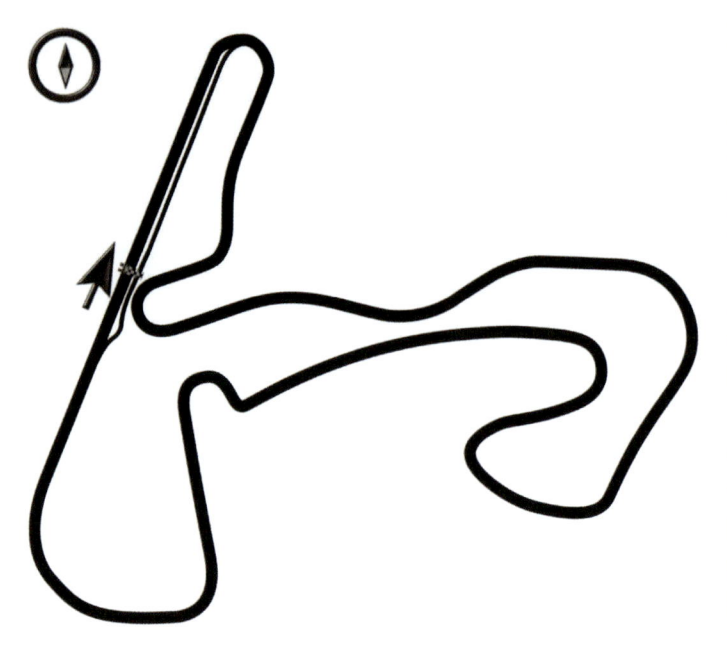

Zandvoort

Capacity	105,000
Length	4.307 Km (2.676 Miles)
Lap record	Not applicable

Zandvoort originally opened in 1948 and held its first F1 Grand Prix four years later.

Formula 1 has not been here since 1985, but returns in 2020 with a new contract.

Since 1985, the southern portion has been shortened and a tight new infield section added, though the Tarzan opening corner, and Scheivlak right-hander are retained.

Zandvoort

Zandvoort is a Dutch coastal town in North Holland, Netherlands, a little to the west of Amsterdam. It is a popular seaside resort, with a long, sandy beach on the North Sea.

Fishing had been the main activity here for many centuries, until the 19th century when it began to be transformed into a seaside resort.

Circling Amsterdam city centre is the Canal Ring, with over 150 canals (more than Venice) and 1,281 bridges. The city is built on swampy, marsh land, so most buildings are supported on wooden poles between 15-20 metres long. Houses typically have 10 poles each, but the Royal Palace has more than 13,500. There are also more bicycles than people.

When going out, note that cannabis may be legal to buy and consume in coffe shops, but smoking tobacco has been banned in cafés and restaurants since 2008.

Poezenboot, also known as Catboat, is the only houseboat in the Netherlands (and possibly the world) for abandoned cats.

Bitterballen (Meatballs)

You will need

Bitterballen: 250g unsalted butter, 125g plain flour, 720ml beef broth, 2 tbsp parsley chopped, 1 small onion chopped, 500g minced beef. ½ tsp salt, 1 tsp black pepper pinch nutmeg.

Breading: 65g plain flour, 3 eggs beaten, 100g breadcrumbs, oil for frying.

Method

Melt butter in a frying pan over medium heat. Add 125g flour gradually, whisking into a thick paste.

Stir in beef broth to make a smooth thick gravy.

Simmer a few minutes. Add parsley, onion, and beef and stir well. Season and add nutmeg to taste.

Cool and refrigerate overnight to solidify.

Set out plates with flour, eggs and bread crumbs. Shape meat mix into 25mm balls. Roll balls in flour, then eggs, then breadcrumbs and repeat until all done. Chill in refrigerator.

Put deep oil in a large saucepan to about 50mm deep. Fry the meatballs 6 at a time until golden.

Serve hot with a grainy or spicy mustard and lager.

Kibbeling (Deep fried fish chunks)

You will need

Kibbeling: 600g white fish, in 5cm chunks, 50g plain flour, 200ml milk, 50ml water or beer, 2 eggs, 1 tsp salt, 1 tsp pepper, portion of fish spice comprised of the following: 1 tsp cinnamon, ¼ tsp cloves, ¼ tsp nutmeg, pinch each of coriander, aniseed, ginger, white pepper and cardamom, all finely ground.

Dips:
Garlic sauce (mayonnaise mixed with finely chopped garlic)
Whisky sauce (mayonnaise, tomato ketchup and a drop of whisky)
Ravigote (if you can buy some).

Method

Mix flour, milk, water/beer, eggs, salt and pepper to make batter.

Heat deep fryer to 170-180C. Put fish in batter, stir around gently.

Carefully slide fish pieces into oil one at a time. Do not overfill the pan. Fry until golden brown, then scoop out with a slotted spoon and place in a bowl lined with kitchen towel.

Cook remaining fish the same way. Scoop out any bits of batter that drop off the fish between batches.

Transfer to serving bowl. Sprinkle with fish spice mix. Serve hot with a dipping sauces.

"Magnussen is, and will always be, stupid!"

Oliebollen
(Dutch doughnuts)

You will need

1 tsp instant dried yeast, 250ml warm milk,
280g plain flour, 2 tsp salt, 1 egg,
115g currants, 115g raisins,
1 apple - peeled, cored and finely chopped,
oil for deep-frying, icing sugar for dusting

Method

Mix the yeast into the milk and set aside for a few minutes. Sift the flour and salt into a large bowl.

Stir the yeast mix and egg into the flour and mix into a smooth batter. Stir in the currants, raisins and apple.

Cover the bowl and leave in a warm place to rise until double in size - about 1 hour.

Heat the oil in a deep-fryer, or heavy deep pan to 190C. Use 2 spoons to shape scoops of dough into balls, then drop carefully into the hot oil.

Fry the balls until golden brown - about 8 mins.

The doughnuts should be soft and not greasy. If the oil is not hot enough, the outside will be tough and the insides greasy.

Drain the cooked doughnuts on paper towels and dust with icing sugar. Serve piled on a dish with more icing sugar dusted over them.

Eat them while still fresh and hot if possible.

Stamppot
(Mashed potato and vegetables)

You will need

2 large red potatoes is 25mm cubes, 1 tbs butter,
60ml milk, salt and black pepper to taste,
1½ tbs olive oil, 1 clove garlic, finely chopped,
1 small onion, finely chopped,
1 small bunch curly kale, chopped in ½-inch pieces,
2tbs water, white wine vinegar,
200g Chorizo thinly sliced,
2 spring onions, finely chopped.

Method

Put the potatoes into salted water. Bring to boil, then simmer until tender, about 10-15 minutes.

Reserve 60ml of the potato cooking water.

Drain potatoes and return to pot.

Add butter and milk and season to taste, then mash the potatoes. For creamier potatoes, add some of the reserved water, a little at a time until you get the desired texture.

In a saucepan, heat 1 tbs oil over low heat.

Fry the onion for 6-7 minutes. Add the garlic and fry 30 seconds, then raise heat to medium.

Add kale, water and a dash of vinegar. Cover and wait 2-3 mins for the kale to wilt. Remove cover and cook 3-4 minutes until kale is tender. Season to taste.

Add kale mix to potatoes and mash thoroughly.

Fry chorizo slices for 4-5 mins. Divide the vegetable mash between 4 bowls. Arrange sausage slices on top. Drizzle with olive oil and sprinkle with the chopped spring onions.

Snert
(Dutch split pea soup)

You will need

1.75 litres water, 300g dried green split peas, 100g pork belly, 1 pork chop, 1 stock cube, 2 sticks celery, 3 carrots, peeled and sliced, 1 large potato, peeled and diced, 1 small onion, chopped, 1 small leek, sliced, 120g celeriac, diced, 1-2 tbs chopped celery leaf, 500g smoked sausage, chopped.

Method

Boil the water in a large pot. Add the split peas, pork belly, pork chop, and stock cube. Cover and simmer for 45 mins, stirring occasionally.

Skim off any foam. Remove the chop, debone it and and thinly slice the meat. Set aside.

Add the celery, carrots, potato, onion, leek, and celeriac. Return to the boil and simmer, uncovered, for about 30 mins, adding extra water if needed.

Add the smoked sausage for the last 15mins.

When the vegetables are tender, remove the bacon and the sausage, slice themthin and set aside.

If you prefer a smooth soup, blend it at this point.

Season the soup to taste. Return the meat to soup, setting some slices of sausage aside.

Serve in bowls, garnished with slices of smoked sausage and chopped celery leaf.

Koolsla
(Classic Dutch coleslaw)

You will need

120g mayonnaise, 1 tsp grain mustard, 1 tsp white wine vinegar, ¼ head each of red and white cabbage, chopped, 2 carrots, grated, 1 leek very finely sliced, 1 red pepper, finely diced, 100g mustard and cress. Optionally, add 100g diced apple and/or 50g chopped walnuts.

Method

Mix mayonnaise, mustard and vinegar for the dressing. Put everything else in a large bowl, add the dressing, and toss well.

Dutch mayonnaise

You will need

230ml sunflower oil, 2 egg yolks, 1 tbs lemon juice, 1 tbs white wine vinegar, 1 tsp Dijon mustard, pinch of salt.

Method

Whisk egg yolks, salt and mustard well until fully combined. Add oil a drop at a time and whisk until it thickens, then slowly add and whisk the rest.

Finally, mix in the vinegar and lemon juice and season. Chill in the refrigerator.

> *"How is the front wing?"*
> *"I don't know -*
> *You'll have to tell me!"*

Italy - Monza

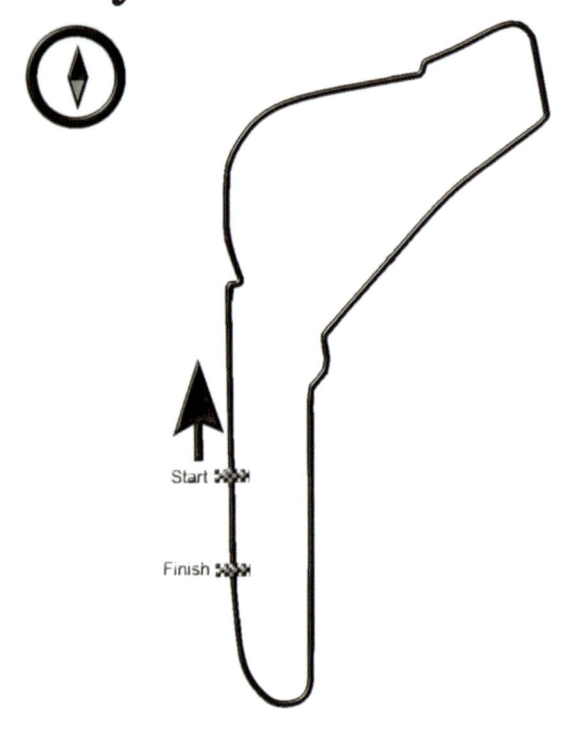

Autodromo Nazionale Monza

Capacity   113,860
Length   5.793 Km (3.600 Miles)
Lap record   R Barrichello (Ferrari) 2004
                81.046 seconds

Monza is known for its long straights and fast corners, which result in full throttle being used for most of the lap.

Low downforce leads to understeer, but oversteer is also a problem in the middle sector. The emphasis is on good straight line speed and traction out of turn one.

Curva Grande down to the Variante della Roggia chicane is the best opportunity for overtaking at Monza.

Monza

The city of Monza is in the northeast of Italy, not far from Milan. It's the third-largest city in Lombardy and important in economic, industrial and administrative terms. There's a large textile industry and publishing trade.

Italian cuisine has influenced food culture around the world. Pasta comes in a wide range of shapes, widths and lengths. In the north, fish, potatoes, rice, sausages, pork and cheese are the commonest ingredients. Pasta dishes with tomatoes are popular, as are many kinds of stuffed pasta, polenta and risotto.

Italians believe that taking a bath when ill will make you sicker. And the number 17 is considered unlucky, so you won't see Italian drivers or teams using it on their cars.

In Milan, an old law requires people to constantly smile while in public places, unless attending a funeral or working in a hospital. And men may be arrested if wearing a skirt in public. So beware any Scots thinking about taking a kilt to Monza...

Arancini
(Deep-fried stuffed rice balls)

You will need

500ml water, 300g short grain rice,
1 tsp saffron, 50g Parmesan, 2 tbs butter,
2 eggs, 150g Mozzarella, diced, 2 tbs plain flour,
4 tbs breadcrumbs, 50g peas, oil for deep frying,
bay leaves. Optionally, 100g minced beef.

Method

Boil the rice in salted water, then cook over very low heat, stirring often, until the water has been absorbed.

If using beef, fry until browned and season.

Dissolve saffron in a little hot water and stir into the rice with the Parmesan. Leave to cool slightly, then add butter and 1 egg and mix well.

Beat the other egg in a bowl and season.

Mould the rice into 10 balls. Press a finger into the centre and fill the cavity with diced cheese and peas, and meat if using. Seal the opening by re-moulding the rice.

Dust each rice ball with flour, then roll in beaten egg, then in breadcrumbs. Fry the ball in deep oil until evenly browned all over. Serve on a plate, garnished with bay leaves.

Spaghetti alla Puttanesca
(Pasta in anchovy and tomato sauce)

You will need

3 tbs olive oil, 1 onion, finely chopped,
2 large garlic cloves, crushed, ½ tsp chilli flakes,
1 can anchovies, 400g can chopped tomatoes,
120g pitted black olives, 2 tbs capers, drained,
300g spaghetti (or other pasta),
small bunch of parsley, finely chopped.

Method

Fry onion over medium heat for about ten mins. Add a pinch of salt plus garlic and chilli flakes. Stir and fry for 1 min.

Stir in the chopped tomatoes, anchovies, olives and capers. Simmer gently for about 15 mins.

Meanwhile, cook pasta in boiling, salted water for about ten mins. Drain pasta.

Stir pasta and parsley into the sauce and mix well.

"Fear is exciting for me"

Panzerotti
(Deep-fried pizza turnovers)

You will need

Dough: 350g bread flour, 125ml water, 100ml milk, 3 tsp sugar, 1 tsp salt, 2 tsp dried yeast.

Sauce: 450g canned tomatoes, chopped, 1 small onion, chopped, 1 stick celery, chopped, 1 tbs tomato puree, 1 tsp sugar, pinch each of garlic powder, dried basil, dried oregano, Dash of lemon juice.

Filling: 100g sliced pepperoni, 450g sliced mozzarella.

Method

Dough: Mix ingredients well and knead for 10-15 mins. Leave to stand in a warm place approx. 30-45mins until doubled in size.

Divide into four pieces and roll each into a thin disc about 18cm in diameter.

Sauce: Simmer ingredients in a covered pan for 20 mins. Sieve or liquidise and season to taste.

Spoon sauce onto the middle of each dough disc. Leave room around edge for sealing when folded.

Top with cheese and pepperoni. Fold over and seal edges.

Heat oil in a deep-fryer or large pan until it is medium hot.

Fry the panzerotti 1 or 2 at a time for 5 mins. Turn over and fry for 5 mins more. Drain well and serve hot with any leftover sauce for dipping.

Fettucini con pollo
(Chicken with fettucini pasta)

You will need

1 tbs olive oil,
100g boneless chicken breast, chopped,
1 small onion, chopped, 1 stick celery, chopped,
1 carrot, chopped, 1 tsp dried oregano,
4 tbs red wine, 225g can tomatoes,
175g fettucine or tagliatelle,
salt, pepper, celery leaves to granish.

Method

Lightly brown chicken in oil. Add onion, celery and carrot. Cook 5 mins until soft.

Add oregano, wine, tomatoes and season. Bring to the boil, then cover and simmer for 10 mins.

Meanwhile, cook the fettucine or tagliatelle in plenty of boiling, lightly salted water until just cooked.

Drain pasta and mix well with the chicken sauce. Serve on a warmed dish, garnished with celery leaves.

> *"I will make sure I hurt myself extra for such a bad day"*

Cannelloni piacentini
(Pasta stuffed with cheese & spinach)

You will need

250g spinach, 100g ricotta, 1 egg yolk,
1 tbs grated Parmesan, ½ tsp nutmeg,
1 tbs chopped mixed herbs (e.g. marjoram, chives, parsley, chervil),
100g cannelloni (see tip),
2 tbs grated Parmesan for sprinkling,
salt and pepper to season.

Sauce: 450g canned tomatoes, chopped,
1 small onion, chopped,
1 stick celery, chopped, 1 tbs tomato puree, ½ tsp sugar, salt and pepper to season.

Method

Wash the spinach and put it into a pan with just the water clinging to it. Cover and cook for 7-10 mins until tender. Drain and chop.

Mix spinach with ricotta, 1 tbs Parmesan, nutmeg, egg yolk, herbs and seasoning.

Preheat the oven to 180C/gas 4.

Stuff the mixture into the cannelloni tubes using a small teaspoon. Lay the stuffed cannelloni in a buttered ovenproof dish.

Simmer sauce ingredients in a covered pan for 20 mins. Sieve or liquidise until smooth.

Pour sauce over cannelloni and sprinkle with 2 tbs Parmesan. Bake uncovered for about 35-40 mins until tender.

Tip: Cannelloni can be awkward to stuff. An alternative is to part-cook lasagne sheets (about 5 mins), drain and cool. Put some filling on a sheet and roll it up.

Salmone con salsa piccante

You will need

2x225g salmon steaks, salt, pepper.

Broth: 150ml dry white wine, 1 bay leaf,
3 sprigs parsley, 1 small onion, chopped,
a few celery leaves.

Sauce: 25g butter, 1 clove garlic, crushed,
1 tbs capers, chopped, 2 tbs chopped parsley.

Method

Season salmon with salt and pepper. Mix broth ingredients in a shallow pan and simmer salmon 12-15 mins on low heat.

Remove salmon and set aside. Strain the broth and set aside.

Fry garlic, capers and parsley in butter for 1 min. Season and add 4 tbs of the broth.

Bring to boil and pour over the salmon. Garnish with a few celery leaves.

Russia

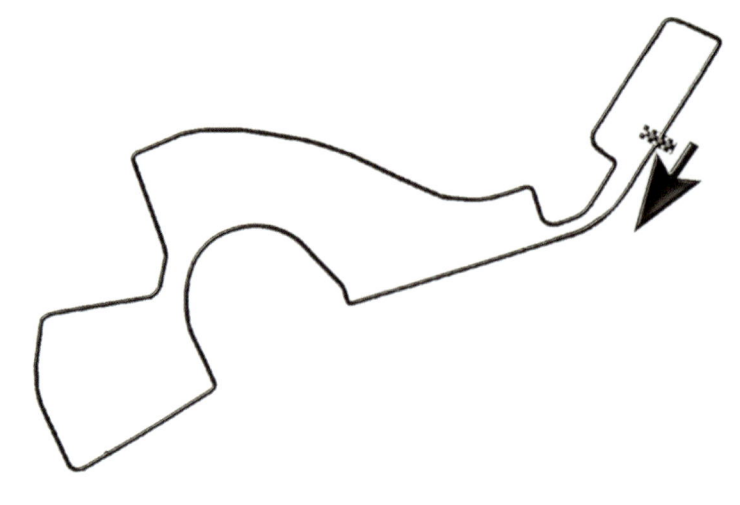

Sochi Autodrom

Capacity	55,000
Length	5.848 km (3.634 miles)
Lap record	L Hamilton (Mercedes) 2019 95.761 seconds

Built around the 2014 Sochi Olympic Park, the first race was held at this track later the same year.

The circuit runs clockwise with 12 right-hand and 6 left-hand corners. Long straights and fast corners make it one of the fastest, with a top speed of 211mph. Even so, it's not a particularly good track for overtaking and there's a statistically high chance of the safety car being needed at some point during the race.

Sochi

The main feature of Russian cuisine is the variety of ingredients. There are lots of dough-based dishes such as pies, cakes, rolls and blini as well as dumplings and noodles. There are many vegetarian favourites such as mushrooms and pickles, too.

On 12th September every year, Russians are given a day off work to have sex. And if they have children nine months later, they are sometimes given cash prizes.

According to recent population statistics, there are 9 million more Russian women than men. Meanwhile, Moscow has more billionaires per capita than anywhere else in the world.

If a chicken crows at you three times before noon, the death of a close family member can be expected within a fortnight.

A stranger should not look at a newborn baby. If one looks at the baby it is bad luck to compliment it. Instead, one could say, 'Oh, what an ugly child!'

Golubtsi
(Stuffed cabbage rolls)

You will need

1 small cabbage, 60g long grain rice,
1 tbs olive oil, 1 onion, chopped,
250g minced beef,
250g minced pork,
2 tbs chopped parsley, 1 carrot, grated,
1 tsp salt, pepper, 2 bay leaves.

Sauce: 160ml chicken stock,
120ml sour cream, 220ml passata.

Method

Top and tail the cabbage and boil in water, gradually removing the leaves as they become loose.

Cook plain rice as shown in appendix. Fry the onions over low heat for 7-10 mins.

Preheat your oven to 180C/gas 4.

Mix beef, pork, parsley, onions, carrots, rice, salt and pepper in a large bowl. Whisk the stock, passata and sour cream in a medium size bowl.

Lay a cabbage leaf on a flat surface and add 2 tbs of filling at the bottom. Roll it up, tucking sides in. Repeat with rest of leaves.

Pour 120ml sauce into a baking dish and arrange cabbage rolls on top. Halfway through add the bay leaves, then continue adding the remaining rolls.

Pour over the remaining sauce, cover and bake for 1 hour. Remove lid and bake 30 mins. Serve topped with sour cream.

Borscht
(Beetroot soup)

You will need

1 cooked beetroot,
1 potato cut into bite-size pieces,
1 tbs oil, 1 small onion, chopped,
1 carrot, grated, ½ cabbage, finely chopped,
½ can kidney beans, 1 bay leaf, 1 litre water,
350ml chicken stock, 1 tbs tomato ketchup,
1 tbs lemon juice, pinch salt and pepper,
½ tbs chopped dill.

Method

Puree ½ the beetroot in a blender, adding a little water if needed. Cut the remaining beetroot into thin sticks. Add beetroot puree to water in a large pan with the potatoes and cook for 10 mins.

Add the cabbage and boil for a further 10 mins.

Fry the carrot and onion in the oil until soft, then add to the pan with the tomato ketchup.

Add the chopped beetroot, chicken stock, lemon juice, pepper, bay leaf, and kidney beans.

Cook 5-10 mins, salt to taste, garnish with dill and serve with sour cream on top.

> *"Ideally there would be a red flag. There is debris everywhere. This track is too fast for this risk!"*

Chebureki
(Deep-fried beef turnovers)

You will need

500g plain flour, 120ml water,
4 tbs olive oil, 1 tsp vodka (optional),
½ tsp sugar, 500g minced beef,
½ onion, chopped, 90ml milk,
1 tbs chopped parsley, salt, pepper,
oil for deep-frying

Method

Sift sugar, pinch of salt and flour in a large bowl. Add oil and vodka. Add water gradually, mixing and kneading to make a soft dough. Add extra flour or water if needed. Leave dough to stand.

Mix beef, onion and parsley, season and stir in milk. On a lightly floured surface, roll dough out to 3mm thick. Cut circles using a small tea plate. Gather leftover dough into a ball, roll and repeat until all is used.

Put 2 tbs filling on one side of a circle, with 15mm to the edges. Fold circle over and pinch edges together firmly. Ensure there is no air inside and edges are closed tightly.

Heat oil and cook the chebureki in batches of 3 or 4 until evenly browned both sides. Drain on paper towels and let stand a few minutes. Serve hot.

Cucumber and radish salad

You will need

2 medium cucumbers, sliced thinly into rounds,
6-8 small radishes, sliced thinly into rounds,
2 spring onions sliced thinly,
120ml sour cream,
2 tbs fresh dill chopped finely,
salt, pepper.

Method

Combine ingredients until the vegetables are coated evenly in sour cream. Serve.

Olivier salad
(Russian potato salad)

You will need

500g cooked chicken, diced,
2-3 potatoes, 2-3 hard-boiled eggs, diced,
2-3 dill pickles (pickled with salt not vinegar),
3-4 tbs mayonnaise, 1 bunch spring onions,
300g thawed frozen peas,
2 carrots, 1tbs chopped dill, salt, pepper.

Method

Boil potatoes and carrots until soft and add peas. Leave to cool to room temperature.

Dice potatoes and carrots and mix in a bowl with the eggs, pickles, spring onions and peas.

Add chicken. Mix well and season.

Add mayonnaise and mix well again.

Sprinkle with dill and chill for 2-3 hours.

"Loads of overtaking is boring"

Kotleti
(Russian burgers)

You will need

200g each of minced pork, chicken, beef,
60g breadcrumbs, 1 small courgette, grated,
1 small clove garlic, 1 egg, beaten,
1 small onion, grated, butter and oil for frying.

Method

Mix everything except the butter and oil in a large bowl. With wet hands, make small meatballs and flatten slightly. Arrange on a baking tray lined with baking paper. Chill for 30 mins to firm up.

Shallow-fry in butter mixed with oil and serve.

Rassolnik pickle soup

You will need

750ml water, 100g beef in bite-size pieces,
1 tbs barley, rinsed, 1 tsp salt, 1 large potato, diced,
1 small carrot, half sliced in rings, half grated,
2 gherkins, diced, 1 tbs olive oil,
½ small onion, chopped, 1 stick celery, thinly sliced,
1 tsp tomato puree, 2 tsp chopped dill, 1 bay leaf,
pepper, sour cream and extra dill to serve.

Method

Boil beef and barley with a pinch of salt for 30 min. Skim off as needed to keep clear.

Fry gherkins for a few mins at medium heat, then add to beef in pot with potatoes and sliced carrots. Cook for 10 mins.

Meanwhile, fry onion for 2 min in oil, add grated carrot and sliced celery and continue to fry until carrots are soft.

Add tomato puree, stir and add to soup pot. Add bay leaf, pepper and dill and season. Simmer until potatoes are soft. Serve with the sour cream and extra dill.

Piroshki
Stuffed savoury bread turnovers

You will need

Dough: 160ml warm water, 45ml warm milk,
1 tsp salt, 1 tsp fast acting dry yeast, 1 tbs sugar,
2 tsp oil, 200g bread flour, plus some for dusting.

Filling: 500g mixed pork and beef mince,
1 tbs oil, 1 small onion, finely chopped,
1 garlic clove, finely chopped, 1 tsp salt,
pinch black pepper, 1 tbs mayonnaise,
2 tbs spring onions, chopped, 1 tbs dill, chopped,
100g butter, cubed, plus the following spice mix:
pinch each of paprika, turmeric, cornflour, onion powder, garlic powder, celery salt.

Method

Mix the dough ingredients and knead well, Leave to rise for about two hours.

Meanwhile, brown the minced pork and beef. Add the oil and onion and fry gently until the onion is tender. Add garlic and spice mix. Fry gently for one minute, then remove from heat and let cool. Mix in the mayonnaise, spring onion and dill.

Once the dough has risen, rollout about 5mm thick and use a glass or cup with a knife to cut into 10cm circles. Collect up the unused scraps of dough and repeat rolling and cutting until all is used.

Put a portion of meat mix into the centre of each circle. Add a small cube of butter on top, then pull up two sides of the circle, pressing together to seal.

Heat oil for deep frying to medium hot, then fry the piroshki one or two at a time until golden, then drain and place on paper towels.

Notes: To reheat, cover and warm in oven. You can also try using a vegetable filling with the same spicing if preferred.

Singapore

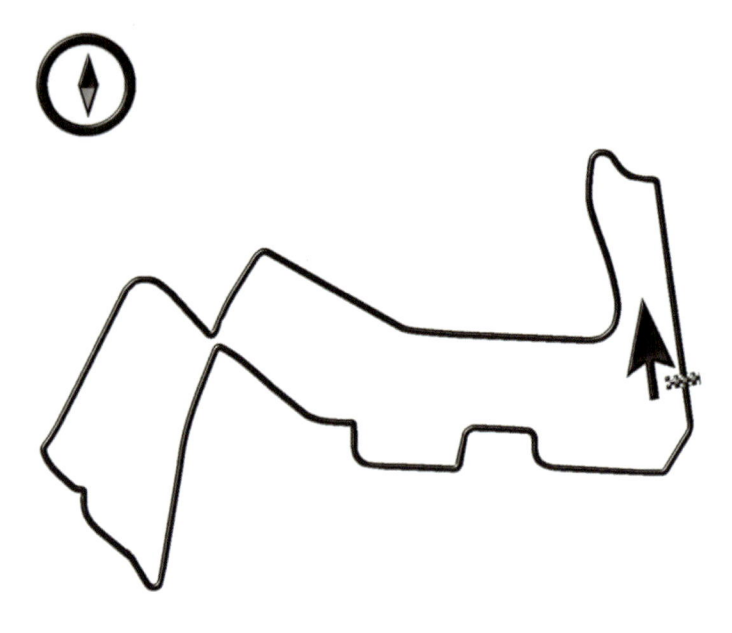

Marina Bay

Capacity	90,000
Length	5.065 Km (3.147 Miles)
Lap record	K Magussen (Haas) 2018 101.905 seconds

When added to the 2008 season, Marina Bay was strongly criticised for having some sections with a very bumpy surface and also excessively high and harsh kerbs.

Changes in the intervening years have fixed most of those issues, as well as 'the worst corner in F1' at the turn 10 chicane and an 'incredibly dangerous' pit entry.

It remains a physically tough track, and F1's only race completely under floodlights.

Singapore

Utilising public roads around the Marina Bay area, powerful floodlights are used to ensure driver and spectator safety.

It's visually spectacular, with sparks from the cars adding much to the effect.

Singaporeans usually refer to older people as 'aunty' or 'uncle'. It's a sign of respect.

Smoking is prohibited in most public areas, on bridges, in hospital outdoor compounds and even within 5 metres of a bus stop.

If you are seen walking around naked at home or in a hotel room, you may face fines or imprisonment on pornography charges. Remember to close the curtains!

Tipping is unnecessary and even frowned upon. At restaurants and cafes, bills will include a 7% Goods and Services Tax and a 10% service charge.

Singing any ballad or obscene song in public is illegal. If you're caught breaking this law, you may be punished with 3 months' imprisonment, a fine or both.

Kanom krok
(Coconut cakes)

You will need

440ml coconut milk, 150g+1-2 tbs rice flour,
1 tbs tapioca flour, 3 tbs desiccated coconut,
40g caster sugar, 1 tbs finely ground jasmine rice,
1 tsp salt, 40ml oil, 1 spring onion, thinly sliced.

Method

Steep desiccated coconut in just enough boiling water to cover for 5-10 mins.

Mix everything except the spring onions well – you may need extra rice flour to make a smooth batter.

Grease and heat a 6-hole Yorkshire pudding pan until it's moderately hot. The batter should sizzle when poured but the pan should not smoke.

Try pouring batter into 1 or 2 holes to test. When hot enough, pour all the batter, cover and cook 5 mins. Cakes should be brown around the outside, but not burnt.

Carefully remove the cakes. If they stick too much, add 1 tbs of rice flour and try again.

Stir the batter again every time you test a batch. Make sure the pan is kept well oiled.

Add a sprinkle of spring onion to each cake before covering. When all are cooked, they should be placed on top of each other to make little 'lanterns'.

Nasi goreng pattaya
(Stuffed omelette fried rice)

You will need

500g cooked rice,
3 shallots or small onions, sliced,
1 clove garlic, chopped,
½ skinless boneless chicken breast, cubed,
50g diced carrots, 50g frozen peas, thawed,
1 tsp tomato ketchup, 2 tsp dark soy sauce,
2 eggs, beaten, salt and pepper.

Method

For the rice: Fry shallots and garlic until fragrant. Add chicken and carrots and stir-fry until cooked.

Add peas and cooked rice and mix well. Season with soy sauce, ketchup, salt and pepper to taste.

Mix thoroughy and set aside.

For the omelette: Season and fry beaten eggs to make a thin omelette. Let the omelette cook and brown at the bottom.

Lay fried rice in the middle of the omelette and spread it out evenly. Fold the edges over into an envelope shape, making sure to enclose the filling and overlap a little.

Transfer omelette to a serving plate. Drizzle ketchup or chilli sauce over the top.

"My game is going wrong – the star is setting"

Hainanese chicken rice

You will need

4 large chicken thighs,
1½ cm cube ginger, finely sliced,
4 cloves garlic, finely chopped,
1 small onion, halved, iced water.

Rice: 350g rice, 1 cm cube fresh ginger, sliced,
2 cloves garlic, sliced,
a few drops each of green food colouring and vanilla essence.

Dipping sauces: 3 fresh red chillies, salt,
juice of 1 lime, 4 cloves garlic, 1 slice fresh ginger or a sprinkle of ground ginger.

Garnish: 1 med cucumber, peeled and sliced,
1 tomato, sliced, 1 tbs light soy sauce,
1 tsp sesame oil, lettuce leaves.

Method

Chicken: Skin and clean chicken, keeping fat to one side. Wash and season chicken inside out.

Add cold water to a large pan and place chicken in the water with onion, garlic and ginger. Season.

Bring to boil and simmer for 20-25 minutes until chicken is cooked.

Remove chicken and plunge into iced water, then drain and dry the chicken and set aside. Strain the chicken stock and set aside. Cut the chicken into bite-size pieces.

Rice: Wash and drain rice. Fry ginger and garlic in reserved chicken fat until fragrant.

Add rice and a little oil to a large pan and gently fry the rice until it is coated with oil.

Add enough chicken stock to cook the rice and the green food colouring and vanilla essence.

Cook until the rice is done.

Dipping sauces: Deseed and grind chillies, adding a little salt, until it becomes a fine paste.

Add a little lime juice and mix well. Put this chilli sauce in a dipping dish.

Chop garlic and ginger very fine and put in another dipping dish.

Arrange lettuce leaves on a serving plate with cucumber slices and tomatoes around the outside.

Place chicken pieces in the centre and drizzle with light soy sauce and sesame oil.

Serve with a bowl of chicken broth, rice and dipping sauces.

"It was that first lap nutcase again"

Chicken satay
(Spicy peanut chicken skewers)

You will need

6 skinless, boneless chicken breast fillets, diced,
2 tbs smooth peanut butter, 7 tsp dark soy sauce,
7 tsp lemon or lime juice, 1 tsp brown sugar,
2 tsp curry powder, 2 cloves garlic, chopped,
1 tsp chilli sauce.

Method

Mix peanut butter, soy sauce, lemon or lime juice, sugar, curry powder, garlic and chilli sauce.

Coat chicken in marinade and refrigerate 2 hours or overnight. Thread chicken onto skewers and grill 5 minutes each side.

Grilled fish with chilli & turmeric

You will need

2 tbs oil, 500g fish fillets, 1 lime.

Chilli paste: 1 clove garlic, 3 shallots,
6 dried chillies, ½ tsp turmeric,
1 tsp fish sauce, 1 tsp sugar, salt.

Method

Blend the chilli paste ingredients in a food processor. Stir-fry chilli paste in hot oil until aromatic. Remove and set aside.

Put fish under a hot grill. Cover with half the chilli paste. Grill about 3 mins.

Turn the fish over, cover with remaining chilli paste and grill the other side.

Remove from heat. Serve with a dash of lime juice.

Chicken curry

You will need

½ chicken, 2 potatoes, 120ml oil,
60g curry powder, 2 onions,
2 stalks lemongrass, 500ml water,
120ml coconut milk, 120ml evaporated milk,
4 tsp salt, ½ tsp sugar, curry leaves.

Paste: 5 cloves garlic, 10 shallots,
3 stalks lemon grass.

Method

Cut potatoes into pieces and deep-fry them in the oil until golden brown. Set aside.

Mix and blend paste ingredients. Stir-fry paste at low heat until fragrant.

Add onions, lemongrass, curry powder and stir, then add chicken, potatoes and water.

Cover and cook until chicken is done.

Add coconut milk, evaporated milk, sugar and salt. Bring to boil, add curry leaves, stir and serve hot.

Japan

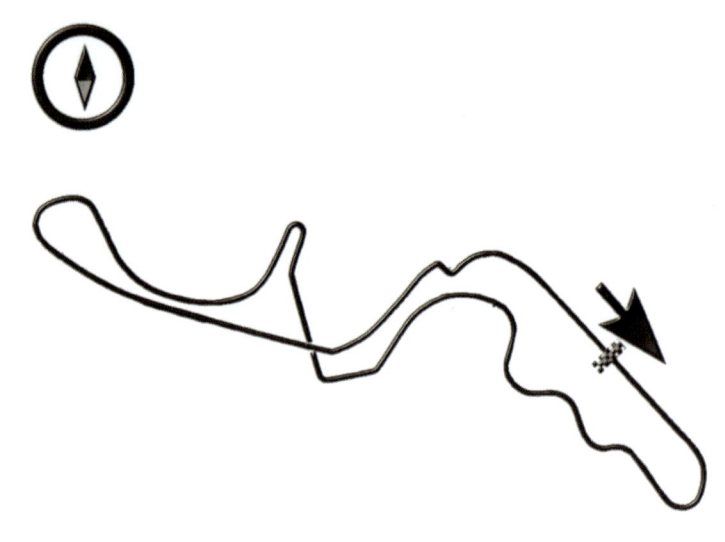

Suzuka International Racing Course

Capacity   155,000
Length   5.807 Km (3.617 Miles)
Lap record   L Hamilton (Mercedes) 2019
             90.983 seconds

Soichiro Honda decided on a permanent circuit in Mie prefecture in the late 1950s.

Designed as a Honda test track, Suzuka is one of few circuits to have a 'figure of eight' layout and is often mentioned by F1 drivers and fans as one of the best of the season.

The final chicane was revised and the 130R corner that precedes it reprofiled in 2003 after Allan McNish had a huge crash during qualifying the previous year.

Suzuka

The number four is to be avoided because it sounds similar to the word for death. It is used as little as possible. Always avoid giving anyone anything in fours because it can be seen as a very ominous gift.

Eating while walking is frowned upon in Japan. Many also consider it rude to eat in public or on the trains.

Slurping is considered polite because it shows you are enjoying your noodles. If you don't eat loudly, it can be taken to mean you are not enjoying your food.

In Japan you are never supposed to pour yourself a drink. If you have poured for others, another guest will pour for you.

'Kit Kat' is similar to the Japanese phrase 'kitto katsu' ('you shall surely win'), used to wish good luck. Students are often given Kit Kat before exams. Japan has dozens of exotic Kit Kat flavours, such as grilled corn, miso, Camembert cheese, baked potato, green tea and soy sauce. So be careful what you buy for yourself.

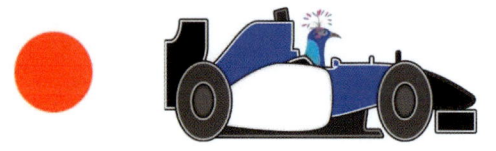

Miso chicken teriyaki
(Pan-fried chicken in savoury sauce)

You will need

200g chicken thigh fillets, skin on,
8 green beans, boiled,
2 tbs miso paste with dashi,
2 tbs water, 1 tsp oil, salt, pepper,
spring onions and plain boiled rice to serve.

Method

Cut excess fat from the chicken fillets and season.

Heat oil in a pan to medium heat and place fillets skin side down. Cook 3-4 mins until skin is browned. Turn over and cook for 5-6 mins until browned.

Mix miso paste with water and spread over the fillets. Add green beans and simmer 2-3 mins until the sauce thickens. Remove from heat.

Slice fillets in bite-size strips. Serve with spring onions and rice.

Note: Miso paste is made from soy beans, cooked to a texture like mashed potatoes.

Dashi just means 'stock' in Japanese and is usually made from seaweed and fish such as flaked tuna, anchovies or sardines in almost any combination of two or more.

These days, miso paste with dashi can be found in larger supermarkets which stock Japanese foods.

Mackerel in miso sauce

You will need

2 mackerel fillets, 2 tbs miso paste with dashi,
1 tbs mirin, 1 tbs sake or dry sherry,
2 tsp sugar, 150ml water,
10g ginger, peeled and thinly sliced,
spring onions and plain boiled rice to serve.

Method

Put ginger, miso paste, mirin, sake, sugar, and water in a saucepan. Stir well and bring to the boil, then reduce heat to low.

Score each mackerel fillet 3-4 times across, then add to saucepan and simmer 15 mins.

Remove mackerel, place on a plate and pour liquid from the saucepan on top.

Garnish with spring onions and serve with rice and a vegetable side dish.

Note: Mirin is a clear, sweet, syrupy liquid. Mirin and miso paste are sold in many large supermarkets.

At a pinch, you can substitute sweet sherry for mirin, though you may need to reduce it down a lot to emulate the effect closely.

> *"I knew I'd been beaten by the best driver in the world"*

Aubergine & green pepper miso stir-fry
(Pan-fried vegetables in savoury sauce)

You will need

1 aubergine, 1 green pepper,
2 tbs mirin, 2 tbs tsuyu stock,
60g miso paste,
30g ginger, peeled and grated,
30g sugar.

Method

Mix everything in a bowl except for the aubergine and pepper to make miso sauce.

Dice aubergine. Slice pepper in thin strips.

Fry aubergine 3-4 mins at medium heat until tender and browned. Add pepper. Fry for 2-3 mins until tender. Add miso sauce and stir well to evenly coat the vegetables.

Serve warm with cooked rice for a light meal or as a vegatable side dish.

Note: Tsuyu stock and miso paste can be found in many large supermarkets.

If you can't find tsuyu stock, you can mix vegetable stock, anchovy paste or Thai fish sauce, soy sauce, mirin or sweet sherry and sugar.

Omurice
(Japanese rice-stuffed omelettes)

You will need (for two omelettes)

½ onion, finely chopped,
1 chicken thigh, boneless and skinless, in 1cm dice,
120g frozen mixed vegetables (defrosted),
salt, pepper, 300-400g cooked rice,
1 tbs tomato ketchup, 1 tsp dark soy sauce,
1 tbs olive oil.

Omelettes: 2 large eggs, 2 tbs milk,
2 tbs olive oil, 6 tbs mature Cheddar, grated.

Method

Fry onion in oil until softened. Add chicken and fry until it changes colour. Add mixed vegetables and season. Mix the rice in well.

Add ketchup and soy sauce, mix thoroughly and transfer the mixture to a warm plate. For the omelettes: Whisk the eggs and milk in a bowl.

Heat a little oil in a pan, ensuring the surface is evenly coated. Pour half the egg and milk mix into the pan and tilt to spread it out evenly. Lower the heat when the bottom of the egg has set. Sprinkle over half the cheese and half the fried rice mix.

Use a spatula to fold the omelette towards the middle, covering the filling. Transfer to warm plate. Decorate with tomato ketchup.
Repeat with the remaining ingredients to make a second omelette.

"It's better to be lost in a big city than in the middle of Siberia"

Chicken Katsu Curry

You will need

120g rice, 2 skinless chicken breasts,
50g plain flour, 2 eggs, beaten,
100g coarse breadcrumbs, 40g mixed salad leaves,
oil for deep frying.

Sauce: 2 tbs oil, 1 onion, finely chopped,
1 clove garlic, finely chopped,
2.5cm cube ginger, peeled and grated,
1 tbs plain flour, 300ml chicken or vegetable stock,
100ml coconut milk, 1tsp light soy sauce,
a little sugar, added to taste,
3 tbs Japanese curry powder or the following:
3 tsp cumin, 3 tsp turmeric, 1 tsp coriander, 1 tsp cardamon, pinch each of fenugreek, nutmeg, cinnamon, allspice, cloves.

Method

Leave the rice to soak in plenty of water while following the steps below.

Stir-fry onions, garlic and ginger on low heat until softened. Add the curry mix and stir gently until fragrant. Add flour and stir for one minute. Add stock gradually, stirring. Add coconut milk, stirring. Add sugar and soy sauce to taste. Blend smooth and keep warm.

Rinse rice well, then drain and put in saucepan with enough water to cover generously. Bring to boil, then turn down to a very low simmer, cover and leave ten minutes. Shake to loosen up, then remove from heat and leave a further ten minutes. Do not remove the cover yet.

Slice each chicken fillet in half lengthways and open out flat. Dredge in flour, then in the beaten egg, then in the breadcrumbs. Deep fry in oil at medium heat until golden and crispy.

Slice cooked chicken diagonally and serve alongside the rice and salad leaves. Pour a generous helping of curry sauce over the chicken.

Hambagu
(Hamburger steak)

You will need

1 large egg, 1 small onion, finely diced,
1 large clove garlic, finely chopped,
450g minced beef, 170g soft tofu,
220ml breadcrumbs, 2 tbs ketchup,
1 tbs oyster sauce, 1 tbs chopped flat leaf parsley,
1 tsp soy sauce, pinch black pepper,
120ml dry red wine, 4 tbs ketchup, 60ml water,
2 tbs tonkatsu sauce.

Method

Fry half the onions and the garlic until well softened and browned. Leave to cool.

Mix beef, tofu, cooked onion and garlic mix, raw onions, breadcrumbs, egg, 2 tbs ketchup, oyster sauce, parsley, soy sauce and pepper until it is evenly textured.

Divide into 8 portions and roll each into a ball, flatten and fry until a dark crust appears. Flip over and brown other side. Repeat for each portion.

When all are done, drain off excess oil and add red wine. Boil to reduce by half. Mix in 4tbs ketchup, water, and tonkatsu sauce.

Return meat to pan. Cover and cook for 7 mins, turning once. Cook uncovered for 3 mins to thicken a little. Serve with rice.

USA

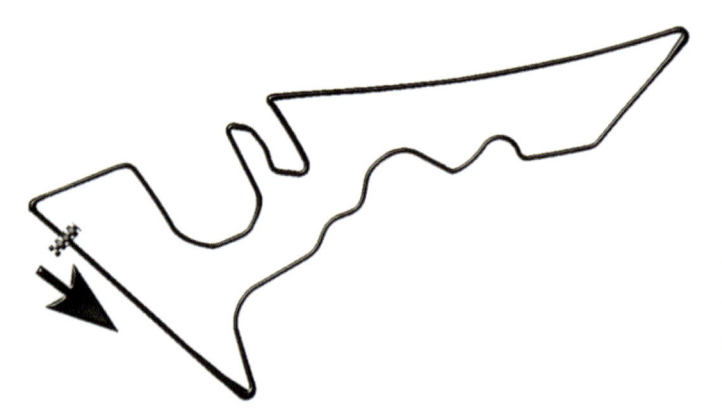

Circuit of the Americas

Capacity   120,000
Length   3.427 Km (5.513 Miles)
Lap record   LeClerc (Ferrari) 2019
                    96.169 seconds

This is a purpose-built track, designed by Hermann Tilke, on 800 acres of land to the east of Austin, Texas. The first F1 race took place here in 2012.

It's a track which is safe but still fun and is probably the best overtaking circuit on the F1 calendar. There are fast corners, a long straight and a slow-speed section, so setting up the car for these different challenges is the key to maximising performance.

Austin

Texas is a big place. Texans love to remind everyone of that. Here are a few odd laws and customs they may not tell you about.

It is illegal to sell one's own eye, or to milk another person's cow. Wire cutters cannot be legally carried in your pocket in Austin.

A recently passed law requires criminals to give victims 24 hours' notice, either orally or in writing, and to explain the nature of the crime to be committed.

It is also illegal to take more than three sips of beer at a time while standing, so be careful while watching the race!

Texans put images of the state everywhere! Not just flags, but t-shirts, bedsheets, toolboxes, tortilla chips, cookies, waffles, coasters and lots more. They also put Jalapeños on everything and like Tex-Mex, BBQ, steak and breakfast tacos.

Texans are also expected to own flip-flops and avoid making reservations of any sort.

San Antonio chilli

You will need

500g beef in 15mm cubes,
250g pork in 15mm cubes,
60g suet, 60g lard,
3 small onions, chopped, 3 garlic cloves, chopped,
500ml water, 2 ancho chillies, 1 serrano chilli,
3 dried red chillies, 2 tsp ground cumin,
1 tbs oregano, plain flour, salt.

Method

Lightly flour the beef and pork. Mix with suet and lard in pan and stir-fry quickly. Add onions and garlic and fry until tender.

Add water and simmer slowly.

Meanwhile remove stems and seeds from chillies and chop finely. Grind chillies with a pestle and mortar, mix with cumin and oregano and salt and add to the pan.

Simmer 2 hours. Skim off excess fat.

Note: In Texas, beans are supposed to be served separately from chillies and meat.

Texas cornbread

You will need

120g plain flour, 120g polenta, lard, 3 tbs sugar,
4 tsp baking powder, salt, 2 eggs, 220ml milk,
1-2 green chillies, chopped.

Method

Preheat oven to 220C/gas 7.

Melt enough lard in a baking dish to cover the base. Place in oven to heat through.

Mix flour, polenta, sugar, baking powder and salt to taste.

Make a well in the middle and mix in the eggs, milk, about 60g lard, and chillies.

Mix well and pour into the pre-heated oven dish. Bake 20-25 mins until browned and cooked through.

Pinto beans

You will need

1 can pinto beans, 50g smoked sausage, chopped,
1 onion, chopped, salt, pepper,
2-3 cloves garlic, chopped.

Method

Mix it all together. Season to taste and simmer until the sauce is thick and brown.

"So if that's legal, then I will do the same next time"

Veracruz prawn cocktail

You will need

100g cooked prawns, peeled and deveined,
1 tbs garlic, crushed, 1 red onion, chopped,
1 jalapeño, deseeded and chopped,
4 tbs chopped fresh parsley, 4 tbs tomato ketchup,
4 tbs lime juice, 1 tsp hot pepper sauce,
4 tbs horseradish sauce,
1 avocado, pitted and diced, salt, pepper.
You also need 350ml clamato juice (branded product, sold in supermarkets), or make your own as follows: mix 300 ml tomato juice, 30ml clam juice or fish sauce, 1 tbs lemon juice, a dash each of chilli sauce and worcestershire sauce, a pinch of celery salt, a pinch of black pepper.

Method

Mix garlic, onion and parsley. Stir in the clamato juice mix, ketchup, lime juice, pepper sauce, jalapeño and horseradish. Season and fold in the prawns. Gently fold in the avocado. Cover and chill for at least 2 hours. Spoon into a chilled cocktail glass.

Green chilli avocado salsa

You will need

2 large green chillies, 500g tomatillos*,
1 avocado, pitted, in half, 3 cloves garlic,
1 bunch coriander leaves, 1 tsp lime juice,
60ml water, salt.

Method

Grill chillies and tomatillos until well blackened all over. Put chillies in a plastic bag and let them steam for 20 mins.

Puree tomatillos in blender. Skin and de-seed chillies and add to blender with everything else.

Puree smooth and add salt to taste.

Bacon-wrapped hot dogs

You will need

10 hot dogs, 10 rashers of bacon,
10 good quality hot dog rolls,
2x pinto beans (recipe on previous page),
3 tomatoes, seeded and diced, 1 onion, diced,
½ bunch coriander, chopped, plus extra to garnish,
2 avocados, peeled and diced, 2 limes, juiced,
220g mayonnaise, thinned with 2-3 tbs milk.

Method

Wrap a rasher of bacon around each hot dog and secure with a cocktail stick. Chill.

Warm the beans. Mix tomatoes, onions and coriander together, then set aside.

Grill bacon-wrapped hot dogs until bacon is crispy, but not burned. Cook slowly, turning often so the hot dogs are heated through.

Mix avocado with lime juice and add to the tomato mixture.

Assemble the hot dogs by spooning beans into a hot dog roll, adding a hot dog and topping with the avocado. Drizzle hot dogs with mayonnaise and garnish with coriander.

*Tomatillos can be hard to find. They're small and green and resemble green cherry tomatoes but are in fact quite different - very tart, yet sweet when roasted. You may find them canned if not fresh.

Ultimate cheeseburger

You will need

Burgers: 500g minced beef, sweet burger buns, 3 processed cheese slices per bun, lettuce, sliced gherkins, mayonnaise, a little butter to spread on the buns, salt and pepper to taste.

Ketchup: 400g can chopped tomatoes, 3 cloves garlic, finely choppod, 1 shallot, sliced, 1 tbs Worcestershire sauce, 2 tbs maple syrup, oil for frying.

Onion rings: 100g plain flour, 2 tsp dried yeast, 150ml lager, salt, 2 large onions.

Method

Ketchup: Mix garlic and salt and grind until smooth. Fry shallot. Mix shallot and tomatoes, Worcestershire sauce and maple syrup. Add garlic mix. Simmer to reduce for about 30-40 mins.

Onion rings: Whisk flour, yeast and salt until smooth. Add lager slowly, whisking until smooth. Set aside for about 1 hour.

Pre-heat a deep-fryer to 170C/medium hot.

Cut onion into thick rings, removing middles. Whisk batter, dust onions with flour and coat with batter. Deep-fry in batches until crisp and golden.

Burgers: Mould beef into eight burgers, about 10 cm diameter. Cook on an oiled griddle or pan for about 2 mins per side, seasoning as needed. Halve a bun, brush with melted butter and toast for a couple of seconds on the griddle or pan.

To serve: spread mayonnaise on bottom half of bun, add lettuce. Add a burger, 2 slices of cheese, a second burger and another slice of cheese, then some gherkin. Spread ketchup on the top half of the bun and use it to finish the burger.

Put remaining ketchup in a small bowl on a plate or board. Place burger and onion rings around the outside.

Mini corn dogs

You will need

30g cornflour, 2 tsp baking powder, 170g polenta, 250g beef hot dogs, each cut across into 3 pieces, 60g plain flour, 2 tbs sugar, 150ml buttermilk, 20 wooden skewers, soaked in water for 30 mins.

Method

Put each hot dog piece onto a skewer. Dredge in cornflour, tapping off excess.

Mix polenta, plain flour, baking powder, sugar and buttermilk in a bowl and whisk until it makes a smooth batter.

Dip each hot dog in batter, coating evenly. Hold the end of the skewer and put the coated hot dog in a deep frying pan of medium hot oil. Fry until golden, 2-3 mins. Drain on paper towels. Repeat with the other hot dogs.

Mexico

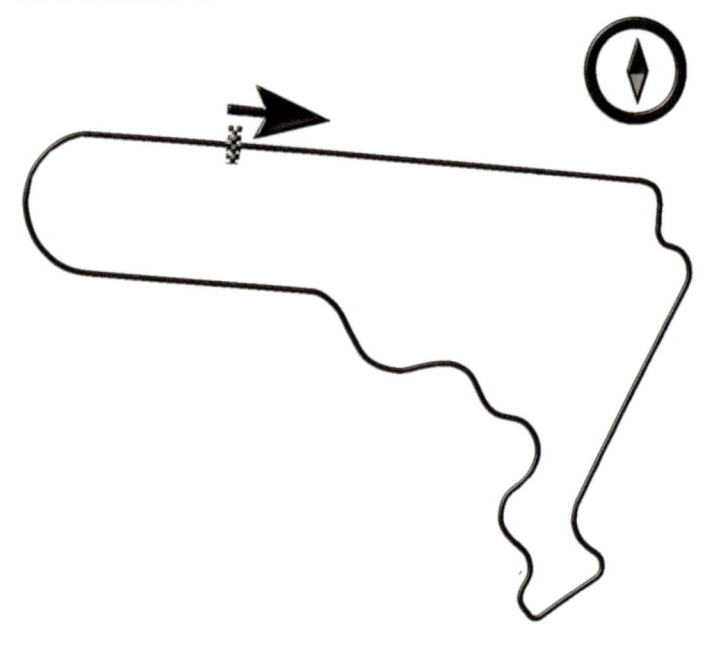

Autódromo Hermanos Rodríguez

Capacity   110,000
Length   4.304 Km (2.674 Miles)
Lap record   V Bottas (Mercedes) 2018
                78.741 seconds

The circuit is in a public park and owned by the city. The surface is very bumpy, due to Mexico City's location in a geologically active region. The high altitude also creates difficulties for both drivers and cars.

The circuit has an extremely fast final turn before a long start-finish straight, similar to Monza, but unlike Monza the final turn is slightly banked, allowing even more speed through the corner. Top speeds of around 230mph occur on the straight.

Mexico City

Mexico City has the second-largest population of any city in the Americas and is the largest Spanish-speaking city in the world. The lifestyle is high density, too.

In Mexico City you cannot drink alcohol in public venues without food, so bars give their drinkers free snacks. Be aware that public toilets seldom provide toilet paper.

When a sauce is described as 'mild', it may not be what you expect. Mild usually just means 'not as hot as the next one'.

Both the Metro and Metrobús have special areas that can only be used by women and there are buses and cabs that only offer their services to women.

In any case, don't expect punctuality. It's considered normal to be 15 or 30 minutes late for any appointment.

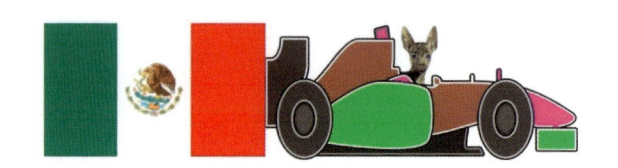

Huevos rancheros (Farm-style eggs)

You will need

4 tbs oil, 4 corn tortilla wraps, 4 eggs,
2x400g cans black beans, drained, juice of 2 limes,
2 ripe avocados, peeled and sliced,
200g feta, crumbled, hot chilli sauce.

Method

Fry a tortilla at high heat 1-2 mins each side until crisp at the edges. Transfer to a plate. Repeat with the other tortillas, then fry the eggs to your liking.

Lightly mash beans in a bowl with fork, adding a squeeze of lime. Spread beans over tortilla and top with egg, avocado, feta and chilli sauce.

Squeeze over lime juice to taste. Serve with a salsa of your choice.

Chicken, mango & jalapeño salad

You will need

250g pack cherry tomatoes, quartered,
2 tbs finely chopped jalapeños, 1 red pepper, sliced,
25g chopped coriander, 1 tbs olive oil,
juice of 1 lime, plus halves to garnish,
1 small red onion, finely chopped,
4 cooked chicken breasts, coarsely shredded,
1 small lettuce, roughly shredded, 1 mango, diced,
tortilla chips, coarsely broken.

Method

Mix tomatoes, jalapeños, coriander, lime juice, onion and oil in a bowl and season. Add remaining ingredients, apart from the tortilla chips and lime halves, and mix.

Sprinkle tortilla chips over the top and serve with lime halves.

Mexican beef chilli

You will need

25g lard, 500g stewing beef, 1 small onion, sliced,
1 tbs chipotle paste, 1 garlic clove, crushed,
10g ginger, grated, 1 tsp ground cumin,
½ tsp ground cinnamon, 1 tsp plain flour,
250ml beef stock, 200g chopped tomatoes,
1 tsp dried oregano,
200g canned pinto or kidney beans, drained.

Method

Brown meat in lard, then set aside.

Fry the onions gently 7-10 mins until caramelised. Stir in chipotle paste, garlic, ginger, cumin, cinnamon and flour and cook 2-3 mins.

Stir in the stock and mix thoroughly.
Add the tomatoes and oregano.

Season and simmer for 10 mins, then add the beef, cover and simmer gently, uncovered, for about 1 hr 30 mins until tender, then add the beans and simmer 15 mins.

If necessary, reduce for 5-10 mins to thicken. Adjust seasoning and serve with bread and salsa.

> *"It was amateur to say the least.*
> *There was no room to pass.*
> *He doesn't seem to like*
> *when a team-mate gets in front"*

Tomatillo salsa

You will need

400g tomatillos*, small bunch coriander,
1 onion, chopped, 1 avocado, diced,
2 green chillies, roughly chopped,
1 garlic clove, roughly chopped, juice of 1 lime.

Method

Cook tomatillos in boiling water for 3 mins until skins split. Drain and cool 5-10 mins.

Mix in food processor with onion, chilli, coriander, garlic and lime. Tip into a bowl, stir in the avocado and season to taste.

*Note: Tomatillos can be hard to find. They're small and green and resemble green cherry tomatoes but are in fact quite different.

Chicken nachos

You will need

200g plain tortilla chips,
2 cooked chicken breasts, shredded,
6 spring onions, thinly sliced,
140g Red Leicester cheese, grated,
sliced pickled jalapeño peppers,
chopped fresh coriander, salsa, hot pepper sauce, yoghurt, guacamole, etc. to serve.

Method

Preheat oven to 200C/gas 6. Layer tortilla chips in a baking dish with chicken, spring onions, cheese and pickled jalapeños. Bake 8 mins or until cheese is melted.

Serve sprinkled with coriander and your favourite accompaniments.

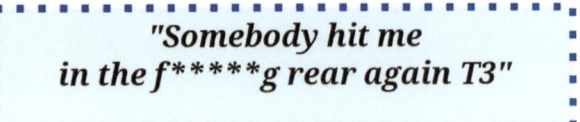

> "Somebody hit me in the f*****g rear again T3"

Spicy vegetable fajitas

You will need

8 white flour tortilla wraps,
2 tbs olive oil,
1 onion, chopped,
1 small cauliflower, cut into small florets,
1 can chickpeas, drained and rinsed,
400g jar arrabbiata tomato sauce,
3 tbs chopped coriander, 150g yoghurt,
50g baby spinach.

Method

Preheat oven to 180C/gas 4, then wrap the tortillas in foil and warm in oven 10 mins.

Fry onion 5 mins in oil until softened. Add the cauliflower and fry 1-2 mins. Add 5 tbs water, cover and cook 5 mins until tender.

Add chickpeas and arrabbiata sauce and bring to the boil. Simmer 2-3 mins, then add coriander and remove from the heat.

You can either assemble the fajitas yourself, or transfer the vegetables to a serving bowl and serve with warm tortillas, yoghurt and spinach so guests can assemble their own

Pulled pork in almond mole sauce

You will need

Pork: 15g lard, 750g pork shoulder, coarsely diced, 1 tsp tomato puree, 200ml chicken stock, zest and juice of 1 orange, 1 stick of cinnamon, 2 sprigs of thyme.

Mole sauce: 2 onions, coarsely chopped, 3 tbs oil, 2 garlic cloves, 250g cherry tomatoes, 2 x 335g packs corn tortillas, 50g flaked almonds, 2 tsp each of ground coriander and cumin, 1-2 tsp chipotle paste, 50g raisins, 25g plain chocolate, finely chopped.

Salsa: 200g radishes, thinly sliced, juice of 2 limes, 2 avocados, chopped, fresh coriander leaves, 1-2 green chillies, finely chopped.

Method

Evenly brown pork in lard for 10 mins, stir in tomato puree and cook 1 min. Add the chicken stock, orange zest and juice, cinnamon and thyme. Bring to the boil, cover and simmer 1½ hrs.

Meanwhile, separately dry cook onions and garlic cloves about 5 mins, turning often, until lightly charred. Transfer to blender.

Add the tomatoes to the pan. Cook 3 mins until starting to blister and char, then add to the blender.

Add 1 tbs oil to pan and fry a tortilla 1 min each side. Tear up and add to blender.

Toast the almonds in a pan for 3 mins until golden. Add to blender.

Gently fry raisins, coriander and cumin 1-2 mins until the raisins swell, then add to blender.

Add chipotle paste and finely chopped chocolate to blender and blend until a rough paste forms. Drain and remove pork from the cooking liquid. Leave to cool, then use forks to tear it coarsely into shreds.

Strain a little of the pork cooking liquid through a sieve into the blender and blend the mixture to a smooth sauce.

Tip sauce into pan with the rest of the cooking juices from the pork and simmer 10-15 mins, then return shredded pork to pan and cook 20 mins more. Season to taste.

The pork in mole sauce can be chilled up to 2 days to save time on race day.

Salsa: Mix all ingredients well and season to taste.

To serve, warm tortillas, spoon some pork onto a tortilla, top with salsa, then roll up.

Brazil

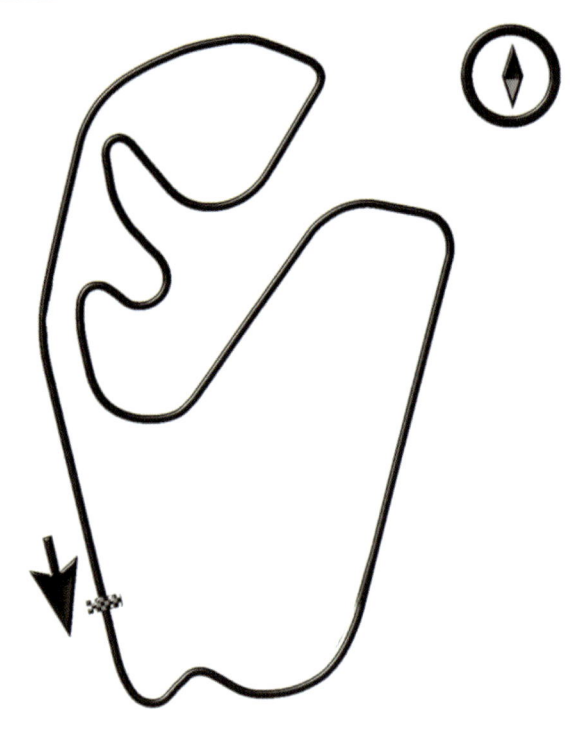

Autódromo José Carlos Pace (aka Interlagos)

Capacity   60,000
Length   4.309 Km (2.677 Miles)
Lap record   V Bottas (Mercedes) 2018
             70.540 seconds

Interlagos literally means 'between lakes' and this geography has often resulted in particularly changeable weather.

The circuit is one of the few to run in an anticlockwise direction, and that combined with high cornering speeds have meant frequent neck strain problems for drivers.

The start-finish straight is also unusual in being uphill, sometimes causing grid issues.

São Paolo

Located in south-eastern Brazil, it's the largest city in the southern hemisphere by population – over 21 million in the greater metropolitan area. It also apparently has the most helicopters in the world.

Brazilians love to touch each other, so don't be surprised when you talk to a Brazilian if they tug at your shirt or wrap their arm around you. It's not a sign of flirtation but a means of friendly communication.

Look out for local character 'Fofão' on the city streets in Sao Paolo. He has injected tons of silicone into his cheeks and got his nickname from a children's TV character.

Women being topless at the beach may be regarded as an offence in Brazil, but public breastfeeding is not.

Most Brazilian municipalities have a law that forbids the use of mobile phones inside banking agencies.

"My rear definitely doesn't feel very good"

Moqueca
(Prawn stew)

You will need

450g large, peeled prawns, 75ml lime juice,
3 garlic cloves, chopped, 3 tbs coconut oil,
4 spring onions, chopped, 1 tsp chilli flakes,
1 onion, sliced in half moons, 2 tsp paprika,
1 red pepper, thinly sliced, 400ml coconut milk,
3 plum tomatoes, deseeded and chopped,
2 tbs chopped coriander, 1 tsp salt,
steamed rice to serve.

Method

Marinate prawns 1 hr in 2 tbs of lime juice, 1 tsp of salt and 1 tbs chopped garlic.

Heat coconut oil and fry spring onion and onion 5 mins, then add red pepper, chilli flakes, paprika and remaining garlic.

Add tomatoes, coconut milk and season to taste. Simmer and reduce 10 mins. Add prawns, marinade and the remaining lime juice.

Gently simmer until prawns turn white, about 3 mins. Serve with fresh coriander and steamed rice.

Feijoada
(Meat and black bean stew)

You will need

400g can black beans,
100g streaky smoked bacon, sliced,
500g pork chops, 3 chorizo cooking sausages,
500g pork shoulder, cut into 5cm cubes,
3 onions, chopped, 4 garlic cloves, finely chopped,
chilli flakes to taste, 2 bay leaves,
2 tbs white wine vinegar.

To serve: steamed rice, chopped parsley or coriander, chilli sauce, orange wedges.

Method

Fry bacon until crisp. Remove, keeping the bacon fat in the pan.

Sear the chops, sausages and pork shoulder in batches, seasoning to taste.

Set the meat aside. Add onion, garlic and chilli to the pan and fry 8 mins or until soft.

Add meat, bay leaves, white wine vinegar and drained beans. Add just enough water to cover. Boil, cover and simmer for 2 hrs until beans are soft and meat is tender.

Season to taste before serving with rice, parsley or coriander, chilli sauce and orange slices.

"I've lost this race, haven't I?"

Chicken coxinha
(Deep-fried chicken parcels)

You will need

175g chicken breast, halved lengthways,
½ onion, 75g full fat cream cheese,
2 spring onions, finely chopped,
1 lime, zest and juice, 1 large garlic clove, crushed.

Dough: 300ml stock from the first step below,
1 tsp oil, 275g plain flour, 1 large egg, beaten,
50g breadcrumbs, salt to taste.

Method

Put chicken and onion in a pan, cover with water, boil, then simmer 10 mins until cooked through.

Remove chicken from pan and leave to cool. Keep the stock. Shred the cooled chicken and mix with the remaining ingredients. Season to taste and chill.

Meanwhile, take 300ml of the stock, strain, add the oil and bring to the boil. Add the flour, stirring vigorously until dough forms. Turn dough out onto floured surface. Season and knead for a few mins. Roll out 3mm thick and cut 10cm circles.

Add some filling to each circle and fold the dough to make teardrop-shaped parcels. Dip each parcel in beaten egg and roll in breadcrumbs to coat.

Heat a deep-fryer to 180C.

Deep-fry the parcels in batches for 5-6 mins until cooked through. Drain and serve warm.

Picadillo
(Minced beef and vegetable hash)

You will need

1 tbs olive oil, 2 cloves garlic, chopped,
1 onion, chopped, 1 small green pepper, chopped,
500g beef mince,
65g green olives, pitted and halved,
45g capers, rinsed and drained,
1 tbs white wine vinegar,
pinch each of salt, pepper, ground cinnamon and ground cloves, 1 bay leaf, dash of chilli sauce,
400g chopped tomatoes.

Method

In a large pan, heat half the oil and fry garlic, onions and green peppers until onions are transparent. Set aside.

In the same pot, heat the remaining oil and brown the mince.

In a separate pan, mix olives, capers, salt, vinegar, pepper, cinnamon, cloves, bay leaf and chilli sauce. Simmer 10 mins.

Add olive mixture and onion mixture to the pot with the mince. Add tomatoes and cook 1 hour over medium heat, stirring.

"It's always maximum attack!"

Pão de queijo (Cheese buns)

You will need

60ml oil, 60ml water, 1 tsp salt,
135g tapioca flour, 1 egg, 5 tbs yoghurt,
40g grated Parmesan, 50g grated Mozzarella.

Method

Preheat oven 180C/gas 4.

Mix and boil oil, water and salt in pan, then pour over tapioca flour in a metal bowl and mix. Beat in the egg, add yoghurt and all the cheese. Pour mixture into mini-muffin tins. Bake 25-30 mins until golden.

Brazilian coconut fish curry

You will need

500g diced haddock, ½ lime, juiced,
2 tsp curry powder, ½ tsp salt, pepper,
1 tsp red food colouring, 1 onion, chopped,
1½ garlic cloves, crushed and chopped,
500ml coconut milk, 1 small tomato, chopped,
1 small pepper, chopped.

Method

Marinate fish with lime juice for 5 mins. Rinse and put in pan. Season with curry powder, salt and pepper. Add red coluring, onion, garlic and 125ml of coconut milk.

Boil, add tomatoes, peppers and remaining coconut milk. Cook 15 mins. Serve hot.

Brazilian fish stew

You will need

3 tbs lime juice, 1 tbs ground cumin,
1 tbs paprika, 2 tsp garlic, chopped, salt, pepper,
675g tilapia fillets, cut into chunks, 2 tbs olive oil,
2 onions, chopped, 4 peppers, sliced,
400g can chopped tomatoes, 400ml coconut milk,
chopped coriander.

Method

Mix lime juice, cumin, paprika, garlic, salt and pepper in a bowl. Add tilapia and toss to coat. Cover and chill 20 mins.

Heat oil until medium hot and fry the onions 1-2 mins. Reduce heat and add the peppers, tilapia and tomatoes in layers.

Pour coconut milk over the mixture, then cover and simmer 15 mins, stirring a few times.

Stir in coriander and cook until the fish is completely cooked through, 5-10 mins.

"Not bad for a number 2 driver"

Australia

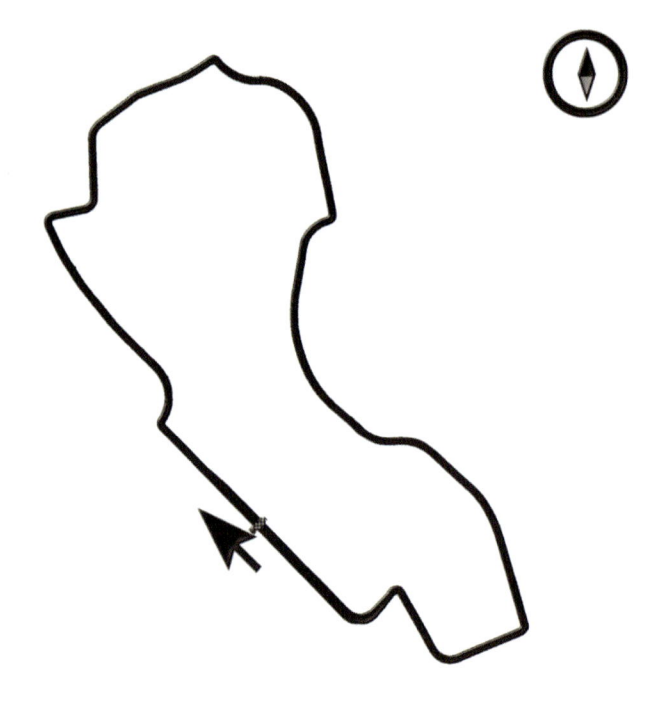

Melbourne Grand Prix Circuit

Capacity   80,000
Length   5.027 km (3.296 miles)
Lap record   M Schumacher (Ferrari) 2004
              124.125 seconds

The original Albert Park circuit was used for Grand Prix in the 1950s, with a revised circuit being introduced for the F1 world championship in 1996.

Although it's a temporary track, using roads around Albert Park Lake, the surface is quite good and it's considered fast and not too hard to learn or drive. Even so, the safety car is often a feature of races here.

Melbourne

Situated on the coast, Melbourne is the capital of the Australian state of Victoria.

The city is divided in two by the Yarra River, which separates the working class areas in the north and west from the more affluent south and east.

The Central Business District (CBD) used to be known as the 'Golden Mile', as it is 1 mile long and ½ mile wide.

Tips for visitors:

Seeding clouds artificially from a manned aircraft in order to make rain is illegal according to the Rain Making Control Act of 1966.

It's also illegal in Melbourne to harness a goat or a dog to a vehicle in a public place.

Only licensed electricians are allowed to change a light bulb, even in a private residence.

Wearing hot pink trousers is illegal after midday on a Sunday, as is dressing up as Batman or Robin.

Finally - probably literally - if you touch electric wires which cause death, you'll get a $200 fine.

"He wants to play bumper cars or something"

Mini chilli beef pies

You will need

450g shortcrust pastry (see essentials),
1 tbs oil, 1 chopped onion, 2 tsp chilli powder,
2 tsp ground cumin, 250g minced beef,
5g tomato puree, 150ml beef stock,
pinch ground cinnamon, 200g can kidney beans,
1 large potato, peeled and diced,
3 tbs sour cream, 2 tbs chopped chives.

Method

Heat the oil to medium and fry the onion until soft - about ten minutes. Reduce heat to low and add the spices. Fry gently for 1 min. or so until they become aromatic.

Increase heat to medium, add the beef and cook for a few mins. until evenly browned. Add tomato puree, stock and cinnamon, then stir and increase heat until it comes to the boil.

Reduce heat to low and simmer until almost dry - about 15-20 mins. Stir in beans and heat through.

Heat oven to 200C/gas 6.

Roll pastry about 3mm thick and cut into twelve circles to line a 12 hole baking tray. Prick the pastry with a fork and bake for 10 mins, then remove from the oven and leave to cool on a wire tray.

Meanwhile, boil potato in water until tender. Drain and mash with sour cream. Season, then stir in the chives.

Spoon 1-2 tsp of chilli mix into each pastry case and top with mash. Return to the oven for 15 mins or until golden.

Variation

Stir strong cheddar or blue cheese into the mash for an extra savoury treat.

Aussie chicken fillets

You will need

4 skinless chicken fillets, 1 tsp salt,
6 rashers bacon, cut in half lengthways,
8 tbs prepared mustard, 8 tbs honey,
4 tbs golden syrup, 4 tbs mayonnaise,
1 tbs dried onion, 1 tbs oil, 70g sliced mushrooms,
270g grated Cheddar, 2 tbs chopped parsley.

Method

Beat the chicken fillets until they are about 1cm thick. Season with salt. Cover and refrigerate for 30 mins.

Preheat oven to 180C/gas 4.

Fry bacon over medium heat until crisp. Set aside.

Combine mustard, honey, golden syrup, dried onion and mayonnaise. Refrigerate half the mixture.

Fry chicken over medium heat for 3 to 5 mins per side until browned. Put the fillets into a baking dish and spread the honey mustard sauce on them. Layer with mushrooms and bacon and sprinkle with grated cheese.

Bake in preheated oven for 15 mins or until the cheese melts and chicken juices run clear. Top with parsley and the remaining honey mustard sauce.

"Aerodynamics is for those who cannot manufacture good engines"

Tasty pea salad

You will need

500g frozen peas, thawed and cooked,
180g can water chestnuts, drained and sliced,
1 red pepper, diced, 125ml plain yoghurt,
2 tsp Dijon mustard, 1 tsp dried dill,
salt and black pepper to season.

Method

Combine peas, water chestnuts and red pepper in a bowl. Mix yoghurt, mustard, dill, salt and pepper in another bowl, then add to peas and water chestnuts and stir to combine. Chill and serve.

Beer can chicken

You will need

1½-2kg good quality whole chicken,
1 tbs olive oil, 1 440ml can lager or similar,
optional mixed herbs and seasonings of your choice.

Method

Heat oven to 180C/gas 4.

Wash and pat dry the chicken, then rub with oil and herbs or seasoning. Open beer, pour off half of the beer, then insert the can in the bird's cavity.

Sit chicken upright on a baking tray and roast for 60-90 minutes, depending on weight. Check juices run clear and roast a little longer if needed.

Don't let the rest of the beer go to waste!

Slow cooked lamb shoulder

You will need

1 shoulder of lamb on the bone to fit your cooking pot or slow cooker,
2 tsp olive oil, 2 carrots,
4 garlic cloves, finely sliced,
2 tbs fresh rosemary, chopped,
250ml white wine, 250ml chicken stock.

Method

You can use a slow cooker or an oven. For an oven, you need a suitable pot with a lid.

Heat the oil in a large frying pan. Season lamb with salt and pepper and brown well all over.

Peel and halve carrots lengthwise and lay in the base of pot or slow cooker.

Sprinkle half the garlic and rosemary over the carrots and top with the lamb, then add the remaining garlic and rosemary.

Return frying pan to heat and add wine. Bring to a simmer, then add stock. Bring back to the boil, then pour over the lamb.

Place baking paper over lamb, put the lid on the pot or slow cooker.

Cook at 190C/gas 5 for 4-6 hours or slow cook at 160C/gas 3 for 6-8 hours.

Meat should be tender, falling off the bone.

Lamingtons
(Coconut & chocolate dipped cakes)

You will need

250g self raising flour, 250g caster sugar,
3 large eggs, 3 tbsp milk, ½ tsp salt
250ml double cream, 2 tbsp icing sugar,
200g raspberry jam, 350g desiccated coconut, 80g unsalted butter, 250ml milk, 50g cocoa powder,
400g icing sugar.

Method

Heat oven to 200C. Grease and line a 20x30cm tin.

Beat butter & sugar until pale and fluffy. Add eggs one at a time and beat well. Add flour, milk & salt and beat until combined. Pour into the lined tin.

Bake 25 mins until firm. Leave to cool.

Slice horizontally and trim edges to make perfect corners, then Cut into 18 squares.

Whip cream with icing sugar until it reaches soft peaks.

Spread a little jam on half the squares, then spread over a little cream.

Sandwich each coated square with an uncoated square, then refrigerate the whole batch.

Whisk melted butter and milk in a bowl. Sieve the cocoa powder & icing sugar in a separate bowl.

Gradually add the cocoa & sugar, whisking to ensure no lumps.

Dip each lamington in icing until covered. Roll in coconut and set on a wire rack. Repeat with the remaining sponges.

Chill for at least 1 hr.

"You've got to push yourself in Formula One; it's not tiddlywinks"

Sweet potato and chive damper
(Easy bread)

You will need

Plain flour for dusting, 400g self-raising flour,
½ tsp salt, 60g butter, (plus extra to serve),
250g sweet potato, 150ml milk,
3 tbsp chopped chives, 3tbsp chopped parsley.

Method

Heat oven to 220C/gas 7.

Mix self-raising flour and salt in a bowl. Rub butter into flour until mixture resembles breadcrumbs.

Peel, chop, boil and mash sweet potato. Mix with milk, chives and parsley. Stir until a sticky dough forms, adding extra milk, if needed.

Turn out onto a lightly floured surface. Knead until smooth. Shape into a 20cm round and put on a floured baking tray. Lightly brush with a little extra milk and sprinkle with salt and pepper. Score top into 8 wedges with a sharp knife.

Bake 30 minutes until golden and it sounds hollow when tapped. Leave to stand for 5 minutes.

Serve warm or at room temperature with butter.

Saudi Arabia

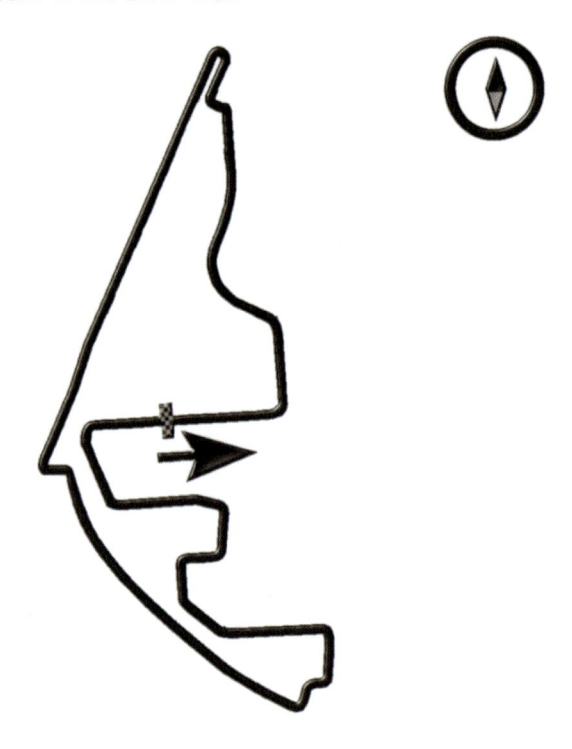

Jeddah Grand Prix Circuit

Capacity	Unstated
Length	5.154 Km (3.203 Miles)
Lap record	None as yet

This is a brand new circuit for 2021. It's a 5.154km street circuit, located near the Jeddah Seaport in Saudi Arabia.

Unusually for a street circuit, it has a purpose-built paddock area, and most common type of corner on the track is a medium-speed sweeping bend.

The last half of the circuit in general has a lot of flow which should encourage a fairly high speed, and provide a unique challenge for drivers.

There is only one DRS zone, on the main straight.

Jeddah

Saudi Arabia is an absolute monarchy - the last significant monarchy in the world. The country has been ruled by the Al Saud family since its birth as a nation on September 23, 1932.

Home to the world's biggest sand desert - the Rub' al Khali - Saudi Arabia has no natural rivers. Even so, there is a shortage of sand for building, so it is imported from other countries, including Australia.

The kingdom also has also the world's biggest water desalination plant.

You can buy gold bars from vending machines.

The Saudi capital is Riyadh, home to the world's biggest camel market, which sells around one hundred camels every day.

The kingdom's oil reserves are huge - more than any other country. Saudi Arabia's Ghawar field is the largest in the world, with an estimated 75 billion barrels of oil in currently known reserves.

Around 47% of the population is aged 24 or under, with only 5% over 60.

The drinking of alcoholic beverages is illegal and a strict interpretation of Islam also prohibits coffee as it is a stimulant, however, the majority of the population does drink coffee.

There is no public transport in this country. People use taxis. However, there is a national health care system in which the government provides free health care services.

Apparently, the "Muppet Show" has been banned because a pig plays one of the main roles.

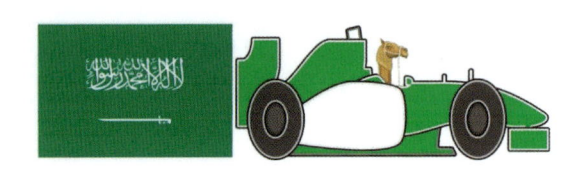

Mutabbaq
Fried pastry square, stuffed with meat

You will need

Dough: 150g plain flour, 1 tsp salt, 1 tbs oil, approx 120ml lukewarm water.

Filling: 1 large egg, 200g minced beef or lamb, 1 tomato, diced, 1 tsp salt, 1 tsp cumin, 1 tbs green leaves from spring onions, chopped.

To serve: Long green chillies, lemon wedges.

Method

Dough: Mix the ingredients thoroughly, adding water very gradually and kneading for about ten minutes to create a firm, not sticky dough. Cover it and leave to rest for at least 30 mins.

Filling: Drop the mince into boiling water for a minute or two, then drain and pat dry.

Add the rest of the filling ingredients and mix well.

Assembly: Roll out the pastry on a oiled board into a very thin square. You should be almost able to see the board through the pastry.

Carefully put the filling into the middle in the shape of a smaller square, a bit less than half the size of the pastry. Fold the pastry over the filling.

Fry in a lightly oiled pan over medium heat for about 3-4 minutes each side. Poke a couple of small holes in the pastry to allow steam to escape if it starts to balloon up.

Serve hot, with the chillies and lemon wedges.

Note: The chillies will be less hot if gently fried or grilled for a few moments, until the skin changes colour. Pickled chillies are milder still.

Dajaj Mashwi
(Arabian grilled chicken)

You will need

4 boneless chicken breasts, 2 tsp Paprika, 1 tsp chilli powder, 1 tsp salt , 1 tsp black pepper, 1 tbsp lime juice, 1 tbsp olive oil

Spice mix: ½ tsp each of cumin, sesame seeds, sumac, dried oregano.

Method

Lightly toast cumin seeds in a dry pan until they are aromatic. Grind finely, then stir in the other spice ingredients, plus a pinch each of salt and pepper.

Pound chicken breasts until about 12mm thick.

Make a paste of the paprika, chilli, salt and pepper with lime juice and rub over the chicken and leave to marinate for about an hour.

Preheat your grill as hot as possible, then grill the chicken breasts for just a couple of minutes each side.

Serve with couscous and dips, e.g.
Humous (see recipe in Abu Dhabi section),

Tzatziki (grated cucumber, mixed with yoghurt, finely chopped garlic and mint leaves)

Tahini dip - tahini or smooth peanut butter mixed to a cream consistency with garlic paste, lemon juice, paprika and olive oil.

Sriracha or chilli sauce - see Essentials section

Baba Ganoush - thoroughly roast an aubegine, scoop out the flesh. Mash with crushed garlic, tahini, lemon juice, olive oil, black pepper and chopped flat leaf parsley.

> *"I just ask you one thing.*
> *If the car becomes dangerous*
> *because of the brakes,*
> *just stop me!"*

Lamb Thareed
(Spicy lamb stew)

You will need

500g diced lamb for stewing, 500ml water,
1 large onion, finely chopped, 1tbs oil,
1tbs tomato puree, 1 vegetable stock cube,
2 cloves of garlic, finely chopped,
1 large potato, quartered, 2 tomatoes, chopped,
1 medium carrot, chopped, 1 pepper, chopped,
1-2 green chillies, 1 tsp lemon or lime powder,
1 tsp cinnamon, 1 tsp turmeric, ½ tsp coriander,
1 tsp hot curry powder, ½ tsp cardamom,
pinch of black pepper,
1 tbs coriander leaves, chopped,
2 small courgettes, halved,
3 large, thin flatbreads, lightly toasted until crisp.
and torn into large pieces.

2 tsp ras-el-hanout ground spice mix:
½ tsp cumin, ½ tsp coriander,
pinch each of cinnamon, ginger, black pepper,
turmeric, cardamom, saffron

Method

Ras-el-hanout: mix together and lightly toast all the spices. Keep to one side, ready for use.

Stew: In a large pot, boil lamb for one hour. Remove any foam. Strain and reserve the stock.

In a large pot, fry onions gently in oil until golden brown. Add garlic and fry for a minute.

Add tomato paste and all vegetables, except the courgettes. Mix well. Add lamb, reserved stock and cube and spices.

Add water if necessary. Season to taste.

Simmer until potatoes are almost done. Add the curgettes and coriander leaves and cook until the courgettes are tender.
Remove meat and vegetables from pot and keep to one side.

In a large, deep bowl, add one layer of bread pieces and spoon over some fo the cooking liquid. Repeat until all the bread is used.

Finally, replace the meat and vegetables ontop of the bread and pour over any remaining liquid.

> *"Ah, finally some points!"*

Chicken Shawarma
(Grilled marinated chicken)

You will need

750g chicken thigh fillets, skinless and boneless
Marinade: 1 large garlic clove, finely chopped, ground spices: 2 tsp coriander, 2 tsp cumin, 2 tsp cardamon, pinch chilli powder, 1 tsp salt, 1 tsp smoked paprika, 1 tsp black pepper, 1 tbs lemon juice, 2 tbs olive oil.
Yoghurt Sauce: 4 tbs yoghurt, 1 tsp cumin, 1 clove garlic, crushed, 2 tsp lemon juice, salt, pepper.
To Serve: 4 pitta bread, crisp lettuce, sliced, 3-4 salad tomatoes, sliced.

Mix marinade ingredients in a large bowl, add the chicken and coat thoroughly. Cover and leave to marinate for at least 4 hours, ideally overnight.

Mix yoghurt sauce ingredients in a bowl. Cover and chill until needed.

Heat grill or BBQ medium high.

Grill chicken each side until nicely charred - about 3-4 mins per side. Put chicken to one side and cover with foil. Let it stand for about 5 mins.

To Serve: Slice the chicken and pile onto a large plate with pitta bread, salad and yoghurt Sauce.

Alternatively, smear a pitta with yoghurt sauce, salad and chicken and roll up.

Jareesh
(Spiced rice with wheat)

You will need

50g rice, 50g crushed wheat (bulgur),
2 large onions, chopped, 250ml chicken stock,
1 tsp cumin, 1 tsp coriander, 1 tsp lime powder,
1 tsp chilli flakes, 100 ml yoghurt, 50g butter.

Method

Wash rice and wheat thoroughly. Set aside.

Fry half of the chopped onion over medium heat in a large pan until soft and translucent.

Add the rice and wheat, stock and enough water to cover. Cover the pan and cook on very low heat until all the water has been absorbed - about 2 hours. Check and stir from time to time.

Fry the remaining onion in butter over a very low heat until dark brown and caramelised. This may take up to an hour or more.

Add the coriander, chilliflakes and dried lime powder to the caramelised onions.

When the rice and wheat have finished cooking, stir in the yogurt, cumin and salt. It should have a creamy consistency, like oatmeal.

If needed, feel free to add more yogurt and salt to taste.

Transfer the rice and wheat mixture to bowls and pour the spiced onions over the top.

Abu Dhabi

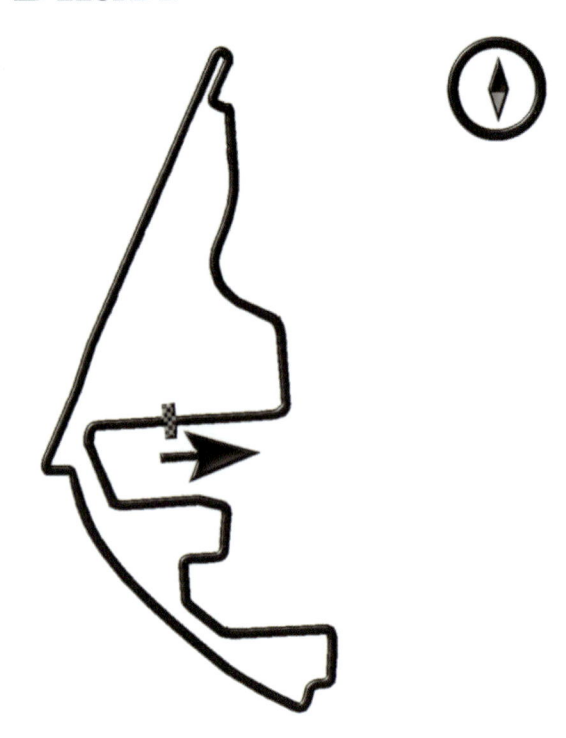

Yas Marina Circuit

Capacity	50,000
Length	5.554 Km (3.451 Miles)
Lap record	L Hamilton (Mercedes) 2019 99.283 seconds

Starting with a medium speed sector with a couple of high speed corners, then a sector with two long straights and two slower corners before a technical final sector, the car must be well balanced to achieve a good lap time.

Tyre management can be a problem, with the early sectors often causing wear which badly affects the car in the later sectors.

Abu Dhabi

The name means 'father of the gazelle' and is thought to be based on the huge number of gazelles in the area.

Historically, Abu Dhabi was a centre for the trade in pearls. The modern city was only planned in the late 1960s and expected to support about 600,000 inhabitants, less than half of the current population, so it's very crowded and congested.

In the UAE, keeping painkillers like codeine and cold or flu medication can result in up to four years' imprisonment.

Unless you're at a licensed club or in the privacy of your hotel room then dancing is considered indecent and provocative and could get you arrested.

E-cigarettes are illegal in the UAE and are likely to be confiscated at the border.

Fattoush
(Bread salad)

You will need

2 flatbreads, 2 spring onions, sliced,
8 lettuce leaves, torn in bite-size pieces,
1 cucumber, diced, 3 tomatoes, cut into wedges,
4 tbs chopped parsley, 1 clove garlic, chopped,
2 tbs sumac, 4 tbs lemon juice, 4 tbs olive oil,
4 tbs chopped mint.

Method

Preheat oven to 175C/gas 4 and toast the flatbreads 5-10 mins until crisp, then break into bite-sized pieces.

Mix bread pieces, lettuce, spring onion, cucumber and tomato in a bowl.

In another bowl, mix parsley, garlic, sumac, lemon juice, olive oil and mint. Season to taste.

Mix with bread salad, toss well and serve.

Shakshouka
(Eggs in spicy tomato sauce)

You will need

4 tomatoes, peeled, seeded and chopped,
4 large green peppers, seeded and chopped,
½ tsp ground coriander, 4 eggs.

Method

Fry green peppers in olive oil until soft, add garlic and cook a few minutes longer.

Add tomatoes and coriander, then crack in the eggs and cook over medium heat for about 10 mins until it thickens. Serve with fresh pitta bread.

Chicken saloona
(Spiced broth)

You will need

1 small potato, 1 baby courgette,
1 small green pepper, 1 small butternut squash,
1 small aubergine, 1 small tomato
and 2 chicken breasts - all diced.
2 tbs chopped coriander, 1 tbs olive oil,
1 small onion, chopped, 1 garlic clove, chopped,
2 tsp fresh ginger, grated, 2 tsp tomato puree,
1 green chilli, finely chopped, 150ml chicken stock, 1-2 pieces dried lime if available,
chopped dill and coriander to garnish
Spices: ½ tsp ground, dried lime, ½ tsp turmeric,
1½ tsp coriander seeds, 2½ tsp ground cloves,
½ cinnamon stick, ½ tsp ground cumin,
1½ brown cardamom,

Method

Heat olive oil and fry chicken for 10 mins, then set aside.

Add potato, courgette, pepper, squash and aubergine to the pan, season to taste and fry 8-10 mins. Set aside.

Fry onion, garlic, chilli and ginger 2-3 mins, add tomatoes, coriander and tomato puree.

Add spices and stir thoroughly. Add the chicken, chicken stock and dried lime and simmer 30 mins.

Add vegetables and simmer 10 mins.

Sprinkle with dill and coriander to serve.

---

*"I just ask you one thing.
If the car becomes dangerous
because of the brakes,
just stop me!"*

Pav bhaji
(Curry in a bun)

You will need

1 tbs oil, 2 onions, chopped, plus extra to serve, 2 tsp finely chopped garlic, ½ tsp chilli powder, ½ tsp turmeric, 1 tsp cumin, 1 tsp coriander, 1 large tomato, chopped, 2 potatoes, diced, 1 carrot, chopped, 50g French beans, chopped, 120g cauliflower florets, 100g green peas, 1 pepper, chopped, 50g butter, 1 tsp garam masala, 1 batch of pav buns (see adjoining recipe), chopped coriander leaves.

Method

Fry onions and garlic paste in oil until soft. Add spices and fry gently for 2 mins. Add tomatoes and cook until soft and mushy.

Add vegetables and mix until evenly coated with spices. Add enough water to cover and simmer until you have a thick sauce. Mash well. Add half the butter and garam masala and mix well. Season to taste.

Split the pav buns horizontally. Add 1 tsp butter to a hot flat pan and toast the buns until they are crisp and golden.

Serve with the filling in a bowl, garnished with butter, coriander and onions.

Pav buns
(Fluffy white rolls)

You will need

250g plain flour, 190ml milk, 1 tsp salt, 20g butter, 3 tsp dried milk powder, 1½ tsp instant dried yeast, 3 tsp sugar.

Method

Warm milk, then add sugar and yeast. Mix well and set aside 10-30 mins.

Mix flour, salt and milk powder thoroughly and make a well in the middle.

When the yeast mixture looks frothy, add it to the dry ingredients and make a dough. It should be quite sticky.

Add butter and knead until the dough is firm – about 15 mins. Transfer dough to a large bowl. Cover and set aside until it has doubled in volume. Knead again for 1 min.

Divide dough into 6 portions. Roll each between your hands to make a ball.

Grease a 20-25cm tin and place the shaped dough balls inside. Keep the balls touching each other.

Cover tin with damp cloth and set aside for another 40-45 mins.

Preheat oven to 200C/gas 6. Brush balls with milk and bake 15 mins until browned.

Finally, brush with butter and leave to cool.

> *"Ah, finally some points!"*

Felafel & hot pepper hummus
(Chickpea rissoles in spicy sauce)

You will need

Hummus: 1 can chickpeas, drained, 2 tbsp olive oil, 60ml lemon juice, 60ml tahini, 1 clove garlic, ½ tsp salt, ½ tsp ground cumin, 2 tbs sriracha or other chilli sauce.

Felafel: 1 can chickpeas, drained, 1 red onion, chopped, 2 tbs pistachios, 100g frozen green peas, thawed, 5 garlic cloves, chopped, 100g parsley, chopped, 50g coriander leaves, chopped, 1 tsp ground cumin, 1 tsp ground coriander, salt, 6 tbs self-raising flour.

Method

Hummus: Put chickpeas, olive oil, lemon juice, tahini, garlic, salt, and cumin in a food processor and mix until smooth, adding olive oil as needed for a creamier hummus. Add pepper sauce and set aside

Felafel: Put all the felafel ingredients into a food processor and mix to a semi-coarse paste. Shape portions of the mixture into golf ball-sized pieces in your hands.

Heat oil in deep pan. Slide one ball of felafel into the oil to test. If the felafel rises to the surface right away, it's hot enough.

Turn gently and cook until evenly browned. Drain on paper towels and repeat with the rest. Serve with the hummus.

Al-motubug
(Stuffed pastry squares)

You will need

375g plain flour, 2 eggs beaten with 2 tbs oil, 1 leek, chopped, 500g minced beef, salt, pepper, 1 small onion, finely chopped.

Method

Mix flour with enough water and salt to make a soft dough. Divide into 8 pieces, knead well and set aside for one hour.

Cook beef, onion, pepper over medium heat until cooked. Season and stir in the chopped leek. Set aside to cool.

Take one piece of dough, roll and stretch until approx. 20cm square and quite thin. Brush egg mixture over the dough and fold in both directions to make a smaller square.

Fry over medium heat until golden brown all over. Repeat with 3 more dough pieces.

Roll and stretch another piece, but before folding, put a fried square in the middle. Cover with beef and egg mixture.

Fold over the filling into a square, brushing egg mixture all over the pastry. Fry over medium heat until both sides are golden brown.

Repeat using remaining pieces of dough to make 4 parcels. Serve hot.

Appendix 1 – essentials

This section includes basic recipes which relate to many different sections of the book as a whole. This just saves repeating the same information many times.

Boiled rice

Rice is enjoyed as a basic side dish all over the world and cooking it is easy, once you know how.

Rather than repeat the method many times, I've put it here, where it can be easily found.

You will need

About 100g rice per person – portion sizes vary from person to person, of course.

Method

Soak rice for a 1-2 hours or overnight.

Rinse thoroughly and drain. Add to a pan and cover with about 1½ times the volume of water. Add salt and a few drops of oil.

Bring to the boil, then turn down to a very low simmer. Cover with a tight fitting lid.

Leave for 10 mins. Shake pan vigorously without removing lid. Remove from heat and leave a further 10 minutes.

Remove lid and fork the rice through to separate the grains. Serve hot or keep to one side for use in other recipes.

Cold cooked rice may be kept in a refrigerator overnight, but extended keeping is not recommended.

Shortcrust pastry

Commonly used for making baked pies, but also for some deep-fried treats, shortcrust pastry is another staple. It's easy enough to get right, and does lots of useful things!

Basic pastry

450g plain flour, 200g butter, pinch of salt.

Alternative pastry

450g plain flour, 1 tsp salt, 2 tsp baking powder, 125g butter, 2 egg yolks.

Method

Mix dry ingredients butter (and egg yolks if using) in a food processor until mixture forms fine crumbs.

Gradually add just enough water to make a firm dough. Wrap dough in cling film and refrigerate for 30-60 mins.

> "We will fight as long as we have gasoline. As long as we have ideals, money, courage, hands, arms, the air we breathe and blood in our veins"

Basic bread dough

This can be adapted in many ways to produce various styles of bread.

You will need

350g bread flour, 225ml warm water, 2 tsp sugar, 2 tbs oil, 2 tsp fast-acting yeast.

Method

Mix everything together in a bowl to form a firm dough. Knead firmly for 10-15 mins.

Leave in a warm place for 30-60 mins, then knead again briefly.

Leave in a warm place for a further 30-60 mins until the volume has doubled.

Preheat oven to 177C/gas 4 and bake the bread for about 45 mins until the top is golden brown and the bottom sounds hollow when tapped firmly with a finger.

Variations

Apart from the obvious such as dividing into rolls, baguettes, etc., you can:

- remove the oil for French-style bread
- use 50% water, 50% milk for pizza
- add egg for a richer dough, but do so by adding water to the egg in a measuring jug so the total volume remains the same
- add seeds of various types while kneading

Chilli garlic sauce

Not really a 'staple' as such, but it adds a fantastic kick to anything. Why miss out?
This recipe makes about 500ml of sauce.

You will need

10-40 chopped red or green chillies (depending how hot you want it),
1 medium onion, finely chopped,
1 medium bulb garlic,
3 tbs wine or cider vinegar,
1 tbs sugar,
3 tbs oil (ideally peanut or sesame),
salt,
jars for storage.

Method

Peel and crush the garlic. Fry lightly in a pan with a few drops of oil. It's done when it has just a hint of colour.

Fry the onion gently until translucent.

Blend garlic, chillies and onions with oil, vinegar and sugar to a smooth paste. Add salt to taste.

Jars for storage should be sterilised. Put glass jars and their lids in cold water and bring to the boil for a few minutes. Alternatively, put a little water in each jar and microwave for a couple of minutes.

Pour or spoon the sauce into jars as necessary.

Keeps for at least a few hours and up to several months in a sealed jar. Once opened, consume within a couple of weeks. Not that that will be difficult!

Appendix 2 - Quote Quiz

You will have seen boxed quotes throughout this book. You were supposed to guess who said which. Here are the attributions, listed alphabetically so you can locate them easily.

"Aerodynamics is for those who cannot manufacture good engines"	Enzo Ferrari
"Ah, finally some points!"	Lance Stroll
"And that is Ralf Schumacher, son of Michael"	Murray Walker
"Are we safe? Can I go for a wee?"	Sebastian Vettel
"Could you describe the conditions around the track please? Errr, fucking wet!"	Lando Norris
"Don't shout, f*****. When I have a chance, but not in the middle of the fast corners"	Kimi Räikkönen
"Don't talk to me through the corners"	Lewis Hamilton
"Driving in Monte Carlo is like riding a bike in your house"	Nelson Piquet
"F*** me that took quite a while that! More than eighty races!"	Valtteri Bottas
"Fear is exciting for me"	Ayrton Senna
"Finishing second means you are the first person to lose"	Gilles Villeneuve
"He's just a total bloody idiot. Always was, always will be"	Derek Warwick
"He wants to play bumper cars or something"	Max Verstappen
"Holy f***, I'm hanging here like a cow!"	Nico Hulkenberg
"Honestly, what are we doing? Racing or ping-pong?"	Sebastian Vettel
"How is the front wing?" "I don't know - you'll have to tell me!"	Kimi Raikkonen
"I am losing one second a lap because of the options. One second!"	Fernando Alonso
"Ideally there would be a red flag. There is debris everywhere. This track is too fast for this risk!"	Fernando Alonso
"If this thing comes off what happens?"	Lewis Hamilton
"I just ask you one thing. If the car becomes dangerous because of the brakes, just stop me!"	Romain Grosjean
"I knew I'd been beaten by the best driver in the world"	René Arnoux
"I'll try to contain my competitiveness so I don't come across like a dickhead"	Daniel Ricciardo
"I'm going to pee in your seat!"	Jenson Button
"I'm such a bastard. I don't ever want to lose the feeling, or let anyone else experience it"	Ayrton Senna
"In sport, there is never any moment that is the same as the other"	Michael Schumacher
"I should have known really that he's mental..."	Jenson Button
"It's always maximum attack!"	Valtteri Bottas
"It's better to be lost in a big city than in the middle of Siberia"	Vitaly Petrov
"It was amateur to say the least. There was no room to pass. He doesn't seem to like when a team-mate gets in front"	Daniel Ricciardo
"It was that first lap nutcase again"	Mark Webber
"I've lost this race, haven't I?"	Lewis Hamilton
"I will drive flat out all the time, I love racing"	Jacques Villeneuve
"I will make sure I hurt myself extra for such a bad day"	Jenson Button
"Just leave me alone, I know what I'm doing"	Kimi Räikkönen
"Loads of overtaking is boring"	Eddie Irvine
"Magnussen is, and will always be, stupid"	Charles LeClerc
"My game is going wrong – the star is setting"	Alberto Ascari
"My rear definitely doesn't feel very good"	Kimi Raikkonen

100

"Not bad for a number 2 driver"	Mark Webber
"Oh, the annoying octopus is back"	Daniil Kvyat
"Racing drivers have balls, unfortunately, none of them are crystal"	David Coulthard
"So if that's legal, then I will do the same next time"	Kimi Räikkönen
"Somebody hit me in the f*****g rear again T3"	Sebastien Vettel
"That's hot air. It's blowing hot air at me!"	Lewis Hamilton
"The car's f****** slow. I can't go faster. It's a piece of s***"	Adrian Sutil
"This is embarrassing, really embarrassing!"	Fernando Alonso
"Unbelievable! I have no idea what just happened. Someone just pushed me"	Felipe Massa
"We need to get it up. I wish I could still get it up"	Bernie Ecclestone
"We will fight as long as we have gasoline. As long as we have ideals, money, courage, hands, arms, the air we breathe and blood in our veins"	Enzo Ferrari
"What a crazy start! What are they doing? They need to calm down"	Fernando Alonso
"What is he doing? Hey! Someone tell him to get a steering wheel!"	Kimi Räikkönen
"You are not giving me useful information"	Fernando Alonso
"You've got to push yourself in Formula One; it's not tiddlywinks"	Mark Webber

Alphabetical index of recipes

Albóndigas	20	Fattoush	95
Al-motubug	97	Feijoada	83
Antipasto della casa	24	Fettuccini con pollo	60
Apple and tuna salad	33	Fisherman's soup	47
Apple, potato and onion hash	32	Flemish frites	53
Arancini	59	Franchesinha Sandwich	17
Aubergine & green pepper miso stiry-fry	72	French onion soup	35
Aussie chicken fillets	87	Fresh egg pasta	11
Austrian potato salad	39	Gazpacho	21
Bacon and Cheddar flan	33	Golubtsi	63
Bacon onion spätzl	41	Goulash	48
Bacon-wrapped hot dogs	76	Green chilli avocado salsa	76
Badimjan borani	29	Grilled fish with chilli & turmeric	69
Badimjan dolmasi	28	Hainanese chicken rice	68
Barbagiuan	25	Ham and endive gratin	52
Basic bread dough	95	Hambagu	73
Beer can chicken	88	Huevos rancheros	79
Beetroot and carrot salad	09	Jareesh	93
Belgian carrots	52	Kanom krok	67
Bifana	16	Kibbeling	55
Bitterballen	55	Koolsla	57
Boeuf bourguignon	36	Kotleti	65
Boiled rice	94	Lamb Thareed	92
Borscht	63	Lamingtons	89
Brazilian coconut fish curry	85	Lángos	49
Brazilian fish stew	85	Lasagne verde al forno	12
Broad beans with ham	20	Lettuce and smoky bacon salad	48
Bubble and squeak cakes	45	Liège salad	53
Caldo Verde	16	Mackerel in miso sauce	71
Cannelloni piacentini	61	Merguez	37
Carbonade flamande or stooflees	51	Mexican beef chilli	79
Canadian baked beans	32	Migas	21
Chebureki	64	Minced meat kebabs	29
Cheese spinach dip	32	Mini chilli beef pies	87
Chicken coxinha	84	Mini corn dogs	77
Chicken curry	69	Miso chicken teriyaki	71
Chicken katsu curry	73	Mortadella, fig and asagio sandwich	12
Chicken machboos	08	Mutabbaq	91
Chicken, mango & jalapeño salad	79	Moqueca	83
Chicken nachos	80	Nasi goreng pattaya	67
Chicken saloona	95	Oignons monégaques	24
Chicken satay	69	Oliebollen	56
Chicken shawarma	93	Olivier salad	64
Chilli garlic sauce	95	Omurice	72
Chunky cod fritters with aïoli	15	Panzerotti	60
Cod baked in foil	40	Pão de queijo	85
Cornish pasties	43	Pasta & Potatoes with Provolone	23
Courgettes with prawns	35	Pastry	94
Cucumber and radish salad	64	Pav bhaji	96
Cucumber salad	48	Pav buns	96
Dajaj Mashwi	91	Peri Peri Chicken with crispy potatoes	17
Dutch mayonnaise	57	Picadillo	84
Easy bannock	31	Pinto beans	75
Escalivada	21	Piroshki	65
Felafel & hot pepper hummus	97	Pissaladiere monégasque	23
		Plaice with grapefruit	35

102

Ploughman's lunch	45
Plov	28
Pork chops in orange sauce	36
Pörkölt with nokedli	49
Portuguese seafood rice	15
Poutine	31
Provençale salad	37
Pulled pork in almond mole sauce	81
Ragù	11
Rakott krumpli	47
Rassolnik pickle soup	65
Roast beef with caramelised onion gravy	44
Roasted parsnip and humous wraps	07
Roasted pumpkin	08
Salmone con salsa piccante	61
Salmon in foil	36
San Antonio chilli	75
Sangria	20
Scotch eggs	43
Shakshouka	95
Slow cooked lamb shoulder	88
Slow-roast tomato, aubergine & feta	07
Snert	57
Socca	25
Sole meunière	51
Spaghetti alla Puttanesca	59
Spanish omelette	19
Spicy vegetable fajitas	80
Squash and aubergine dip	09
Stoemp	52
Stamppot	56
Sweet chilli pork belly tapas	19
Sweet potato and chive damper	89
Tasty pea salad	88
Texas cornbread	75
Tiroler gröstl	40
Tomaten kohl	41
Tomatillo salsa	80
Tortellini al brodo	13
Toyug kebabs	27
Ultimate cheeseburger	77
Veracruz prawn cocktail	76
Watermelon and feta salad	07
Waterzooi	52
Wiener schnitzel	39
Yellow split pea soup with ham	31
Yellow rice with meat	09
Yoghurt and herb soup	27
Yorkshire puddings	44

Printed in Great Britain
by Amazon